Information Literacy for Today's Diverse Students

Information Literacy for Today's Diverse Students

Differentiated Instructional Techniques for Academic Librarians

Alex Berrio Matamoros

LIBRARIES UNLIMITED™
An Imprint of ABC-CLIO, LLC
Santa Barbara, California • Denver, Colorado

Library of Congress Cataloging-in-Publication Data

Names: Berrio Matamoros, Alex, author.
Title: Information literacy for today's diverse students : differentiated
    instructional techniques for academic librarians / Alex Berrio Matamoros.
Description: Santa Barbara, California : Libraries Unlimited, [2019] |
    Includes bibliographical references and index.
Identifiers: LCCN 2018031624 (print) | LCCN 2018035652 (ebook) |
    ISBN 9781440862083 (e-book) | ISBN 9781440862076 (pbk. : acid-free paper)
Subjects: LCSH: Information literacy—Study and teaching (Higher) |
    Academic libraries—Relations with faculty and curriculum. |
    Individualized instruction.
Classification: LCC ZA3075 (ebook) | LCC ZA3075 .M39 2018 (print) |
    DDC 025.5/677—dc23
LC record available at https://lccn.loc.gov/2018031624

ISBN: 978-1-4408-6207-6 (paperback)
        978-1-4408-6208-3 (ebook)

23 22 21 20 19   1 2 3 4 5

This book is also available as an eBook.

Libraries Unlimited
An Imprint of ABC-CLIO, LLC

ABC-CLIO, LLC
130 Cremona Drive, P.O. Box 1911
Santa Barbara, California 93116-1911
www.abc-clio.com

This book is printed on acid-free paper ∞

Manufactured in the United States of America

Portions of this book are reused from Berrio Matamoros, A. (2016). Differentiated Instruction in Information Literacy Courses in Urban Universities: How Flipping the Classroom Can Transform a Course and Help Reach All Students. *Urban Library Journal*, 22 (1). Retrieved from http://academicworks.cuny.edu/ulj/vol22/iss1/1.

To Solana, Kaia, Ellie, Mairi, and Carlos,
who inspire me to always look for
opportunities to become a better educator

Contents

ONE

Overcoming the Limitations of Traditional Teaching Methods with Differentiated Instruction

INTRODUCTION

The dominant approach to teaching in colleges and universities employs at-home readings and in-class lectures to introduce students to new material, followed by written assignments and exams designed to assess how well students acquired the intended knowledge from a course. This traditional instruction approach takes a one-size-fits-all view of teaching and learning, where instructors prepare lectures, select readings, and design graded assessments with the intention of making sure the average student has the greatest opportunity to succeed in his or her learning, inevitably leaving some students struggling to make sense of the material while the most advanced students often feel unchallenged. This approach also ignores the facts that students come to a course with different levels of knowledge regarding the topic and prior exposure to the material, that they have different interests that they are curious and passionate about, and that the way they best learn varies because of innate learning styles, environmental preferences, gender, cultural backgrounds, and life experiences that impact how they perceive what they are learning and how they interact with instructors and with their peers. If an educator considers it a priority to give all students the best opportunity to learn and master what is taught, this traditional instruction approach leaves much to be desired.

In recent years, instructors in higher education have begun following the lead of primary and secondary school teachers in moving away from the traditional approach to teaching. Oftentimes instructors are motivated to make changes after learning about the impact that differences in learning styles have on how students best process and understand new concepts and information. They might replace a reading assignment with a video that covers the same content, assign a group project instead of a written assignment, or make other changes that better accommodate students whose learning styles differ from those who prefer to listen to lectures, read textbooks, and write reports or essays. Another trend is to incorporate active learning in the classroom, where students engage with the material through discussions and debates, problem-solving exercises, or other activities that allow students to think about what they are learning, make sense of it, and check whether they truly understand it. These types of changes can improve the learning experiences of some students but may have the unintended consequence of disadvantaging those who prefer the traditional approach.

In addition to differences in learning styles, readiness, and interest among students enrolled in undergraduate and graduate programs, their backgrounds have grown more diverse by every measure, whether it be race, ethnicity, nationality, gender, socioeconomic status, or other aspects of one's identity. Together with this increase in diversity comes greater variety in students' cultural norms and cultural expectations that influence how they interact with instructors and peers. These norms and expectations, along with a student's life experiences, have been shown to also impact how a student learns. The impact of cultural diversity on learning will be explored in Chapter Two.

With so many differences in learning styles and backgrounds among students that affect how they take in, process, and master new course material, it may seem nearly impossible for the most well-intentioned instructor to design a course to accommodate these differences in order to maximize each student's opportunity to successfully learn. The aim of this book is to make this laudable goal achievable for all academic instruction librarians who teach information literacy by introducing them to a differentiated instruction teaching approach, explaining the approach and its benefits for students of all learning styles and cultural backgrounds, and offering practical guidance for its adoption in information literacy courses and one-shots.

When instruction is differentiated, students are not limited to only one way to engage with new material, make sense of what they are learning, test their own understanding, and eventually show the instructor how well they have learned what was taught. Instead, students are given at least two options to choose from at each step in the learning process with the expectation that one will better suit their learning style and learning preferences. Information literacy courses contain the flexibility needed for differentiated instruction because much of the course content does not necessarily have to be delivered in-class for students to understand it. The suitability of the approach for information literacy instruction is bolstered by the fact that most courses already contain in-class exercises or other active learning experiences that are a core component of differentiated instruction.

The limitations of a traditional instructional approach for accommodating several learning styles are explored in this chapter before introducing differentiated instruction (often interchangeably referred to as differentiation) as a solution to those limitations. In Chapter Two, the impact of cultural diversity on learning is discussed. Guidance for preparing to differentiate instruction is offered in Chapter Three, including the presentation of several reasons to consider adopting a flipped classroom instructional approach in conjunction with differentiation in order to maximize the benefits of both approaches. In Chapters Four, Five, and Six, the necessary preparations for each phase of differentiated instruction are explained, along with summaries of a multitude of tools and techniques to consider using when designing instructional materials. The final chapter focuses on the implementation of differentiated instruction in information literacy courses and one-shot sessions.

As a way of providing realistic context for the planning and implementation of differentiated instruction, a scenario is introduced at the end of this chapter involving a library professor endeavoring to differentiate a first-year undergraduate information literacy course for the first time. Accounts of the professor's consideration, preparation, and eventual implementation of differentiated instruction appear throughout several chapters. Three of the culturally diverse students in the course are introduced in Chapter Two, and their experiences with differentiation are presented alongside the later detailing of the professor's implementation.

LIMITATIONS OF TRADITIONAL INSTRUCTION FOR ACCOMMODATING VARIOUS LEARNING STYLES

A number of learning style models describe how students best learn based on personal traits that determine how they perceive new information (perceptual models), absorb and retain new information (cognitive models), process information and form ideas (also cognitive models), or their attitudes and behaviors when learning (affective models) (Coffield, Moseley, Hall, &

Ecclestone, 2004; James & Gardner, 1995; Zapalska & Dabb, 2002). The differences between perceptual, cognitive, and affective models are easiest to understand using examples from each category.

A well-known perceptual model—Fleming and Mills's visual, aural, read-write, and kinesthetic (VARK) model—places learners into one of four groups depending on the sensory pathway or modalities they prefer for engaging with new information (Jacobson, 2001). Visual learners best understand information presented using images, diagrams, illustrations, and videos. Aural learners, sometimes called auditory learners, prefer hearing new information in lectures, discussions, and narrated videos. Receiving new information through text is the preferred way for read-write learners to learn it. Kinesthetic or tactile learners prefer active learning experiences, where they get to do something with the information they are learning, such as problem-solving exercises and delivering presentations.

David Kolb's experiential learning theory, a cognitive model, emphasizes the experience one goes through when learning new information. It contains two complementary elements, a four-stage learning cycle and four learning styles, based on how a learner both perceives new information and processes it (Kolb & Kolb, 2005). Kolb's learning cycle consists of two stages where learners perceive new information in some way and two stages where they process it. Each learning style reflects a learner's preference for one of the perception stages and one of the processing stages.

The learning process ordinarily requires more than one trip through Kolb's learning cycle as learners refine their understanding of new information. The four stages, referred to as modes by Kolb, of the learning cycle are described here and represented in Figure 1.1:

- *Concrete Experience:* A learner actively participates in a new experience or reinterprets an existing experience. Two learners may perceive the same experience differently based on their feelings, personal views, and past experiences.

- *Reflective Observation:* A learner processes the experience by reflecting on it, taking into consideration one's observations and perceptions, as well as the impact it had on the learner.

- *Abstract Conceptualization:* Based on the logical analysis of reflections and observations, a learner forms ideas and theories to explain the experience and then draws conclusions about it.

- *Active Experimentation:* The learner plans ways to test the newly formed ideas and theories with the goal of revising what one knows and understands. These plans are then put into action.

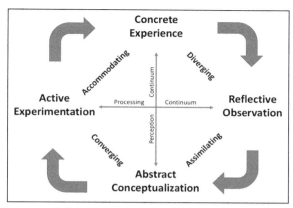

Figure 1.1 Kolb's Experiential Learning Cycle and Learning Styles

There is no preset starting point for everyone on Kolb's learning cycle because different types of learners prefer to begin at different modes depending on individual variations in cultural background, identity, life experiences, and the demands of one's present situation or environment. For example, some learners may prefer to actively participate in a new experience they encounter, while others may want to first observe.

Each learning style in Kolb's theory reflects a learner's preference for one perceiving and one processing mode, resulting in four learning styles, as noted in the quadrants of Figure 1.1 and described here (Kolb & Kolb, 2005):

- *Diverging:* These learners prefer concrete experimentation and reflective observation. They excel at looking at experiences from many different perspectives and generating new ideas. They prefer to learn by working in groups, listening with an open mind, and receiving personal feedback.

- *Assimilating:* Abstract conceptualization and reflective observation are the preferred modes of individuals with this learning style. These preferences align with their desire to learn by exploring analytical models and taking time to analyze new information and also reflect their heightened ability to understand a wide variety of information and arrange it logically. A traditional instruction approach focused on readings and lectures suits them best.

- *Converging:* These learners' preference for abstract conceptualization and active experimentation leads them to outdo others at finding practical uses for ideas and theories and excel at completing technical tasks. They learn best by experimenting, participating in simulations, and applying what they learn in practical situations.

- *Accommodating:* The dominant learning abilities for these individuals are concrete experimentation and active experimentation. They depend on others to provide them with information and conclusions following analysis, rather than engaging in the logical analysis themselves. They prefer to learn by setting goals, testing different approaches, working with others to complete assignments, and engaging in hands-on experiences.

An example of an affective model is the Grasha-Riechmann Learning Style Scales, which uses three pairs of attitudes and behaviors to describe students' social interactions related to learning: avoidant or participative, competitive or collaborative, and dependent or independent (Grasha, 1990). Participative students enjoy learning and fully involve themselves in all learning activities, tending to prefer the traditional instruction model. Avoidant students show no interest in attending class or engaging with the content. Competitive students are motivated by performing better than their peers, become more stimulated when competing against others, prefer a teacher-centered instructional approach, and tend to dominate in-class discussions. Collaborative learners prefer to work with others to share ideas in small-group discussions and accomplish tasks through group projects. Dependent students show little intellectual curiosity and rely on others for guidance about what to learn and how to learn it, preferring instructors to give clear assignment instructions and provide topic outlines and notes. Independent learners are confident of their abilities and prefer student-centered instruction that allows them to work alone at their own pace.

Deconstructing these three learning style models raises a number of considerations for an instructor seeking to accommodate how various students best learn. One should think about how students' senses are taking in and working through what is taught, how they experience it, how they logically analyze it, how they reflect on past learning experiences, whether they are actively making sense of it or expecting others to give them the analytical conclusions, their degree of interest in learning, their preference to collaborate or compete, and their desire to work independently or not. If the traditional lecture-read-write instructional approach is examined in the context of the VARK model, it satisfies the needs of aural and read-write learners.

As previously mentioned, students with an assimilating learning style in Kolb's model are best accommodated by traditional instruction's focus on allowing the learner to analyze new information and to explore analytical models at their own pace, outside the classroom. As for the Grasha-Riechmann model, traditional instruction favors competitive learners over collaborative ones because of the absence of collaboration and also best accommodates participative and dependent students who benefit most from teacher-centered instruction, while disadvantaging independent students who would prefer self-paced instruction over having to learn at the same pace as their peers.

Overcoming the limitations of traditional instruction by accommodating the many aspects of how students learn may seem overwhelming, and it certainly can be without proper planning. Methodically adopting differentiated instruction or components of it allows instructors to offer students choices that best suit the ways they learn. An introduction to differentiated instruction and an exploration of the research into its effectiveness follow, with guidance on planning for and implementing the approach presented in Chapter Three.

OVERCOMING THE LIMITATIONS OF TRADITIONAL INSTRUCTION WITH DIFFERENTIATED INSTRUCTION

Differentiated instruction is a student-centered teaching approach that acknowledges that every student learns differently because of variations in individual readiness, interests, and learning profile. A student's readiness encompasses prior knowledge, life experiences that may offer unique insights into new material, and cognitive and metacognitive abilities. The passion students feel for their strongest interests or their curiosity about developing interests can help motivate them in their learning. Learning profile describes factors that impact one's preferred way of learning, such as learning style, cultural background, gender, and environmental aspects, such as noise level, activity level, and furniture arrangement (Santangelo & Tomlinson, 2012). The term "learning profile" is often used in discussing differentiated instruction because it is the preferred term of Carol Ann Tomlinson, the foremost expert on differentiation. Although this book focuses mostly on the learning style and cultural background factors that contribute to learning profiles, other factors will be mentioned and discussed in the portions of the book where they are most relevant.

In order to address these variations and engage all learners, instructors who differentiate offer students choices for how they take part in the various phases of the learning process in order to best offer every student an opportunity to succeed at learning what is expected of them. Differentiation can also involve offering choices for different classroom environments, such as setting up one area of a classroom with desks where students are facing one another to facilitate group work, while another area has individual desks where students may sit quietly, with headphones or earplugs, to work alone. Because differentiating a classroom can be more difficult to accomplish in colleges and universities where most classrooms are shared, this aspect of the approach will not be emphasized in this book, although opportunities to differentiate the classroom environment will be noted when they arise.

Differentiated instruction is not a step-by-step teaching model but rather an approach or philosophy where instructors can combine a variety of teaching strategies, techniques, and tools to expand the options related to how students receive course content, make sense of what is taught, test their own understanding, and show the instructor that they have acquired the desired skills and knowledge. Allowing students to choose among learning objects—the items you provide them to assist in their learning—gives them the opportunity to find what best suits how they learn. Although differentiation is a student-centered approach, teaching and learning remain an instructor-led process, with the expectation that students will be more responsible for their own learning. Differentiated instruction is best understood by examining how a student's learning process moves from the initial delivery of course content through the eventual mastery of that content.

Content Delivery

Content Delivery, often shortened to "Content" when talking about differentiated instruction, refers to the conveyance to students of the information, ideas, and skills that they are expected to learn. Some instructors describe Content through the use of learning outcomes or objectives, the summary or list of what a successful student will know in the end. The first aspect of differentiation is offering students choices for how they initially engage with the Content. In traditional instruction, course Content is delivered through in-class lectures and at-home reading of textbooks or articles. In differentiated instruction, students have additional learning object choices, such as videos, audio recordings, multimedia presentation slides, interactive tutorials, or options that vary based on students' level of readiness.

Process

Process is the way that students make sense of the Content and acquire the knowledge expected of them. In traditional instruction, this may happen when a professor asks a question in class that requires students to synthesize what they are learning, when reading assignments contain questions that prompt the reader to think through and analyze that Content, or when students are studying on their own. More often than not in a traditional approach to learning, Process is the invisible step between first engaging new Content and producing a final Product that shows mastery, leaving students to make sense of the material on their own. Differentiation is perhaps most valuable to them in this step because they are given new tools to help bridge the gap between taking in new information and turning it into knowledge and skills that they can then show to the instructor. This can be done through whole-class or small-group discussions, debates in the classroom, online discussion boards, in-class exercises, or other learning activities and experiences.

Product

In differentiated instruction, the Product learning objects are the assessment devices students complete to show their understanding of the Content and to demonstrate their acquisition of relevant knowledge. In traditional instruction, this is most often done using a written Product, such as an essay, report, or exam. Sometimes students are given ungraded quizzes or practice tests as formative assessments to assess their own understanding and to gauge their progress toward mastery of the Content. With differentiation, students are given the choice of additional ways of showing they have acquired the expected knowledge and have satisfied learning outcomes or objectives; an example is the option to create presentation slides to answer a question, to record video or audio of them explaining an answer, or to design a flowchart that shows their reasoning as they work their way to the answer.

RESEARCH ON THE EFFECTIVENESS OF DIFFERENTIATION

Research into the effectiveness of differentiated instruction in higher education is limited because the approach has only recently begun to catch on beyond primary and secondary education. In one mixed-methods study involving 39 undergraduate education majors enrolled in two sections of a math course, both sections did equally as well on a pretest given at the start of the semester and seemed to be beginning on fairly equal footing. In the differentiated section, students were assigned to one of three groups depending on their performance on the pretest. Each group was then given a menu of options for Content, Process, and Product that varied by group. Students in all three groups were required to participate in a group presentation at the end of the unit, with no differentiated choice given. The students in the differentiated section scored higher on the final exam by an average of 20 points out of a possible 200 compared to the control section, a statistically significant difference. In an end-of-semester survey, many students credited differentiation with giving them more face-to-face time with the instructor, but several thought that the work involved took up too much of their time (Butler & Van Lowe, 2010).

Another study followed students in an undergraduate educational psychology course where a control section of 38 students receiving traditional instruction was compared to a differentiated section with 39 students, where instruction included hands-on activities and students were given choices for completing assignments, with the instructor modifying the teaching plan midsemester based on formative assessment results. Six graded assignments and three exams were administered to both sections. The differentiated group performed better on five assignments but to a statistically significant degree only on two. When the six assignment scores were combined, the differentiated section significantly outdid their traditionally taught peers. Similarly, on all three exams, the differentiated group scored higher, although to a statistically significant level on only one exam. When considering all three exams in aggregate, the differentiated sectioned significantly outperformed the other section. Students in the differentiated section also commented that they believe they learned the material at a deeper level, valued having choices when completing their assignments, appreciated doing self-reviews as a formative assessment, and felt that the course was "a fit" for them (Dosch & Zidon, 2014).

In a qualitative study of student feedback from a college foundations of education course where instruction was differentiated primarily through small-group work, researchers identified recurring themes, such as the majority of students expressing that they found the course more interesting, interactive, attention holding, and enjoyable than traditional courses. Some students were critical of the additional out-of-class time required to complete the active learning exercises, and a few expressed dissatisfaction with being required to engage in some group work (Livingston, 2006).

A mixed-methods study administered the Student Instructional Report (SIR) II, a standardized course evaluation instrument with well established reliability and validity, in order to evaluate student perceptions of how differentiation affected their learning in an undergraduate education course. Students found that their learning increased significantly compared to traditional instruction and that the quality of instruction positively impacted the learning process. Students felt challenged but supported and saw the course as actively involving them in their learning. In students' narrative responses, they expressed finding differentiation beneficial because college students have diverse ways of learning; they have diverse interests, experiences, and goals; and they have diverse personal circumstances. Students expressed great support for having the ability to choose activities and assessments that they believe best suited their learning styles. They reported that having options "increased motivation to put forth effort, enhanced understanding and internalization of the concepts, and created a desire to pursue additional, independent learning," along with "an increased sense of voice and personal agency in the class." The researchers, who were also the instructors, noted "that the time, effort, and dedication required for effective differentiation is [sic] unequivocally worthwhile when the high level of student engagement and mastery are [sic] experienced" (Santangelo & Tomlinson, 2009, p. 320).

In a mixed-methods study that took place in an undergraduate first-year math course at two universities, five sections of the course were differentiated and five sections were taught traditionally as the control group. The instructors used a wide variety of differentiated instruction techniques throughout the semester, offering choices to students for Content, Process, and Product to accommodate students of varied readiness, interests, and learning profiles. All students were given a pretest at the beginning of the course, and the same test was given on the last day of class (posttest). Students in the differentiated sections saw a greater rise in their scores from pretest to posttest when compared to the control group and viewed the course more positively due to the use of differentiated instruction. The researchers, who were also instructors in the course, found it helpful to identify the learning objectives for the course early on in planning differentiation and to use them to help make decisions about which units to differentiate and what approaches to take. They also found it helpful to keep in mind that it was not necessary to differentiate every class or every assignment (Chamberlin & Powers, 2010).

WHAT DIFFERENTIATED INSTRUCTION IS NOT

Although differentiated instruction focuses on the fact that students learn differently, it is not individualized instruction where a custom curriculum is created for each student based on individual needs and abilities. In differentiation, students are given options, but it is their responsibility to choose the option that best suits them. The up-front preparation and design of various options may be time-consuming for the instructor, but, once they are created, they can be reused in future courses rather than having to create or redesign learning objects for individual students.

The approach should not be thought of as a way to accommodate students with learning disabilities or below-average academic abilities, although this may be an additional benefit of adopting differentiated instruction. The approach is not about differences in abilities but about differences in student readiness, interest, and the ways they learn. Preassessment, discussed in Chapter Three, helps instructors identify these differences for each student. Understanding variations in learning styles and the influence that one's personal background can have on the learning process is a critical step in preparing for differentiation, which is why it is explained in the first two chapters of this book.

Differentiated instruction is also not synonymous with active learning. Active learning is a component of differentiation, but just offering learning activities to help students make sense of the Content, without offering variety for Content Delivery and assessments, falls short of the goals of differentiation. Attempting to offer students choices in Content, Process, and Product is the hallmark of differentiated instruction.

Differentiation is also not exclusively about making changes to what happens inside the classroom or exclusively about what work students do outside the classroom, but it must involve offering choices that support the learning that happens in both locations. Adopting the approach may mean that the time spent in the classroom may be noisier and a bit rowdy, but it is not an unmanageable free-for-all. Undergraduates and graduate students are adults, and they should receive the benefit of the doubt that they can behave themselves and understand that, by being given choices, they are more responsible for directing their own learning and should be respectful of the classroom as a learning environment. Differentiated instruction has been successfully adopted in K–12 education for decades, and adult learners should be expected to be able to behave appropriately in a classroom if children are able to. The buzzing of activity may at first feel like chaos for an instructor accustomed to a quiet environment, where students take lecture notes and maybe write an assignment or complete a worksheet alone at their desks, but remember that this is a sign that students are actively working to make sense of what they are learning. Suggestions and tips for managing a differentiated classroom are offered in Chapter Three.

CHALLENGES OF DIFFERENTIATING

You may be thinking that if you offer students choices like those just mentioned, the teaching, learning, and assessment phases of instruction will be overly time-consuming and difficult to manage. Without proper planning, creativity, and an openness to being flexible as an instructor, it could become challenging. But by following the practical guidance offered in this book and allowing yourself plenty of time to plan, the effort put into giving students choices should pay off when they truly understand and learn the material and are able to demonstrate that when completing summative assessments.

One common mistake is to attempt to differentiate an entire course without any prior experience with the teaching techniques you choose to adopt. When you first introduce an unfamiliar teaching technique or tool into your course, you are a learner and need to give yourself time to experiment, observe whether it works well for your students, and grow accustomed to it. The explanations in Chapter Three of how to use different tools and techniques are designed to make your learning and execution easier. Consider incorporating differentiation into your teaching slowly by introducing changes in only one or a few units of a course at first, adding additional differentiated learning objects each time you teach the course. This gradual approach can improve the chances of success and lower the stress of implementation. Because differentiated instruction is an approach or philosophy and not a firm model, making some changes but leaving other sections of a course the same will work.

Another challenge is to take time to reflect on what went well, what did not, and how things could improve. Ideally, all of the new learning objects created for your differentiated portions will be created well in advance. But many instructors find themselves in a situation where they are pressed for time to create new content, activities, and assessments because it is close to when the lessons will take place, and often they do not take the time to reflect on the impact that differentiation is having on students. Although students' performance on assessments may be your main focus, it is important to reflect on whether students seem more interested in and engaged with the material and to observe whether they are putting more effort into completing their assignments. Students who show more interest and make more of an effort in their learning ordinarily retain more of that knowledge for the long term.

As you follow a hypothetical academic instruction librarian, Prof. Lee, through the process of adopting differentiated instruction over the next several chapters, you will learn how she addresses these and other challenges along the way.

THE HYPOTHETICAL: PROFESSOR LEE'S INFORMATION LITERACY COURSE

Prof. Lee is an academic instruction librarian who teaches a first-year undergraduate information literacy course in the fall semester each year at a suburban community college. She took one course on information literacy instruction during her master's in library science program but had very limited teaching experience when she began, having led only a few research one-shots before teaching her first course under the supervision of an experienced instruction librarian. Over the 15 years Prof. Lee has taught the course, she has read much about pedagogy and learning styles and has attended webinars and workshops to broaden her knowledge of teaching techniques and tools. She has made some changes to the course to appeal to different learning styles, such as assigning some vendor-created video tutorials on using certain research databases and replacing one written assignment with a multimedia assignment where students are expected to use PowerPoint or other presentation software to create a presentation on a course-related topic of their choosing that is due on the last day of class.

She has wanted to make more changes to her lesson plans and assignments to accommodate students with different learning styles but has noticed that some of the students who do well on traditional written assignments are not doing as well on the presentation assignment, and she's conflicted by the possibility that making changes will disadvantage those students while benefiting others. Recently she has begun exploring the idea of differentiating at least some of the lessons for a few course topics after coming across the approach, while trying to learn more about accommodating learning styles. She has decided to differentiate the units of the course that focus on search strategies and critically evaluating sources.

Prof. Lee has also noticed that, in recent years, her classroom of 25 students contains more racially and ethnically diverse students now than when she first began, along with having a larger number of students who are immigrants or the children of immigrants. These students interact with her differently in the classroom and office hours compared to her white middle- and upper-class students, and she has begun reading about how cultural differences affect the way students learn. She is committed to creating the best learning environment for all her students to succeed in developing the information literacy knowledge and skills she is teaching them, but she wants to be sure that any changes she makes are fair to all students and do not disadvantage any one group.

On the first day of class Prof. Lee administers a preassessment based on the Information Competency Assessment Instrument developed by Rodney Marshall (Marshall, 2006) in order to gauge the students' familiarity with the Content covered in the course. New to the questionnaire are three final questions related to interests and learning styles:

21. I would like to include some examples in the course related to students' career plans and personal interests. Please share whatever you are comfortable with below.

22. How do you think you best learn? Consider things like what happens in the classroom, what you do for homework, how you make sense of what you are learning, and how you study. Think about lectures, readings, activities, taking notes, organizing your thoughts, and the environment around you.

23. Which of the following are learning activities that you think would work best for how you learn?

    A. Reading textbooks and articles
    B. In-class lectures
    C. Streaming videos I create instead of lectures
    D. Podcast/audio versions of lectures with accompanying PowerPoint slides

E. In-class group work

F. In-class debates

G. Individual activities in the classroom

H. Ungraded, online practice quizzes

I. Quick reflections written at the end of class

Prof. Lee feels a bit awkward asking students about their personal interests, even though she intends to use this information to better engage them, which is why the first question on the preceding list is phrased carefully to invite students to write down whatever interests they are comfortable sharing. She includes the next question to find out about her students' learning styles and their awareness of how they best learn. She plans to use this information to help decide how to differentiate learning objects in the course and to help determine possible groupings of students for small-group activities. She has identified a few Content, Process, and Product techniques and activities that she feels comfortable experimenting with during the two differentiated units and shares those learning objects in the final question for students to check off from a list. She has already decided that students will have differentiated options for how they prepare the final project but has not yet determined exactly how this will work.

She schedules 10-minute meetings with each student in the first two weeks of class to talk about their experience with using different research tools and also to get to know them and learn more about how they think they best learn. She believes that these conversations will help her build a rapport with each student that will be especially valuable during the two differentiated units where she will be spending some time working with students in small groups and possibly individually.

In the next chapter, we will meet three of the students in Prof. Lee's class and follow them in later chapters to learn about their experience with differentiated instruction in the information literacy course.

TWO

The Impact of Cultural Diversity on Learning

THE INTERSECTION OF CULTURE AND LEARNING STYLE

Culture is not exclusively tied to race or ethnicity but also includes "shared motives, values, beliefs, identities, and interpretations or meanings of significant events that result from common experiences of members of collectives that are transmitted across generations" (House, Hanges, Javidan, Dorfman, & Gupta, 2004, p. 15). Research has shown that the one-size-fits-all traditional teaching approach excludes students whose cultural backgrounds differ from the majority and inhibits efficient and effective learning (Wynd & Bozman, 1996) because those students engage course content differently (Packard, 2011).

Researchers studying the interaction of culture and learning style share five common assumptions about learners (Guild, 1994, pp. 18–19):

1. Learners in different age groups differ in how they learn.
2. Both nature and nurture impact one's learning style.
3. Learning styles are neutral, meaning that adapting instruction to a particular learning style can be successful for some students but can also be a barrier to learning for other students.
4. Learning styles cannot be generalized to apply to an entire group of people with a common culture because, as much as there are common traits within a group, there are also numerous differences.

5. There are often cultural conflicts between some students' socialized behavior at home and the cultural norms imposed on them at school, forcing them to adapt to the classroom norms in order to succeed academically.

Examining the first of these five assumptions from the perspective of an academic instruction librarian, instructors can expect that most students will be close in age, although there may be some outliers. For the second assumption, "nature" can be thought of as a student's innate learning preferences, motivation to learn, and cognitive abilities. "Nurture" closely correlates to the influence that cultural identity and life experiences have on one's learning style and also includes a student's degree of interest in the material. The third assumption speaks to Prof. Lee's concern that if she makes changes to portions of her course to accommodate a certain learning style, students of other learning styles will be disadvantaged.

The fourth assumption is arguably the most important to keep in mind while reading this chapter and thinking about the impact that cultural differences have on how students learn. The studies summarized in this chapter show that some variants in learning styles can be tied to students' cultural backgrounds, but this association is not a generalization for the entire cultural group. For the purpose of considering differentiated instruction as a response to the impact of cultural diversity on learning, keep in mind that decades of research involving students at all grade levels, along with observations made by thousands of teachers, provide strong evidence that differences in students' varied cultures can be great enough to impact how they learn. The evidence from these studies and observations merit an instructor's attention when considering how to best reach all learners.

The final assumption provides the most convincing reason for why differentiated instruction should be considered as a way to address how cultural differences affect some students' learning styles. Students who experience a conflict between their culture and the norms they are expected to adhere to in the classroom are forced to expend effort on acting as two different people with two different sets of behaviors in order to perform well academically. This can be mentally and emotionally exhausting for students and harm their chances at academic success. In some cases, meeting the expectation of conforming to the cultural norms of the classroom can cause students stress and anxiety that interfere with their learning if the process of adopting those norms does not come easily.

Similar to the research on differentiated instruction, more emphasis has been placed on studying the impact of cultural diversity on learning in primary and secondary education than in higher education. However, several cross-cultural studies examined whether differences in learning styles exist between college or graduate students from different countries working on degrees in the same field in their home country. One study compared Australian, Hong Kongese, and Taiwanese accounting students using Kolb's Learning Style Inventory (Auyeung & Sands, 1996). The researchers found that students from Chinese cultures (Hong Kongese and Taiwanese) were significantly more likely to show traits attributed to the assimilating learning style, where learners prefer reflective observation and abstract conceptualization, compared to Australian students. These learners were less action oriented and relied more on reflections about an experience and their observations during it. The researchers attributed these traits to the expectation in Chinese society that individuals prioritize group goals over personal concerns. In contrast, Australian students, predominantly of British descent, mainly displayed traits of accommodating learners, preferring participation in concrete experiences and active experimentation. This learning style and the associated traits were attributed to the high value placed on self-reliance and individual achievement in Anglo-Australian society. This study also showed that no single learning style was dominant for accounting students across countries but seemed to depend on cultural background. As stated in the preceding fourth assumption, these differences cannot be generalized to apply to all students from a particular cultural group. They should be used only to show that certain learning style traits are more likely to be found in one culture when compared to another.

A nine-year study of 7,300 undergraduates from 81 countries enrolled in the same course at one university explored how their learning-related dispositions differed (Tempelaar, Rienties, Giesbers, & van der Loeff, 2013). In addition to learning styles, "learning-related dispositions" include implicit theories of intelligence, effort beliefs, academic motivation, achievement goals, and learning attitudes. The researchers administered several assessments of learning-related dispositions, including one based on Hofstede's six cultural dimensions, a framework for cross-cultural communications used to examine cultural differences. The first dimension, power distance, measures the expectation by less powerful members of a group that an unequal distribution of power will exist in the group. Next, uncertainty avoidance measures group members' tolerance for uncertainty and ambiguity. The third dimension, individualism versus collectivism, indicates whether a group operates with loose ties among members, with the expectation that members care for themselves and their family, or strong ties among members, where there is a supportive, integrated collective. Fourth is the masculine-feminine dimension of a culture, where individuals in masculine cultures have distinct emotional gender roles, such as men tending to be assertive and focused on success, while women are expected to be tender and focused on quality of life, in contrast to feminine cultures where both genders display the stereotypical feminine traits. The fifth dimension measures whether a society values fulfillment of present needs more than future rewards (long term versus short term), while the sixth measures indulgence in human drives that lead to the enjoyment of life versus cultural restraint that regulates gratification by strict social norms (Tempelaar et al., 2013).

Studies by Hofstede and others using his framework have identified differences between nationalities along the six cultural dimensions. This nine-year study found that cultural differences had a small effect on learning style but that those differences had a greater impact on students' motivation for learning and also on the degree to which these students were focused on succeeding in learning. The researchers also examined correlations between each of Hofstede's six dimensions and other elements of students' learning-related dispositions and found that students from individualistic societies, such as the United States, showed many learning-related disposition traits inverse to those from collectivist societies like China. Similarly, those from cultures that were different on the indulgence versus restraint and masculinity versus femininity dimensions had many differences in their learning-related dispositions. Cultural differences related to uncertainty avoidance and to long term versus short term also showed some weaker correlations.

Other studies administered learning style assessments to employees raised in different countries but doing the same job in the same industry. One such study used Kolb's Learning Style Inventory to identify the learning styles of Japanese managers for multinational corporations on multiyear overseas assignments in the United States and compared them to American managers in the same corporations (Yamazaki & Kayes, 2007). The Japanese managers were grouped by how long they had worked in the United States: less than one year, one to less than two years, two to less than three years, and three or more years. Japanese expatriates mostly showed a diverging learning style with a preference for concrete experience and reflective observation. On the other hand, the American managers displayed a preference for abstract conceptualization and active experimentation, indicative of a converging learning style. Japanese managers who had spent longer periods working in the United States started showing an increasing preference for active experimentation like their American counterparts, pointing to the possibility that exposure to a different set of cultural practices in the workplace can eventually lead to changes in learning traits.

The results of these studies suggest that learning styles are not independent of culture. The correlations may not always be strong or definitive, but they are statistically significant and should not be overlooked when considering how to accommodate differences among how students learn. Whether it be adopting attitudes about learning imparted by members of their community or assuming expectations about classroom behavior commonly held by people in their nation of origin, these outside influences can cause students to modify their learning behaviors from an early age to conform to norms from one or more aspects of their background. For students who come from a close-knit family where nearly every task involves two or more people, the idea of working on something entirely independently feels foreign to them. If learning to cook at home involves practicing a dish over and over again without ever writing down the recipe because that is how cooking is traditionally learned in their culture, it may be difficult for some students to succeed academically if they are only given written information about what they must learn and never get to actively engage in making sense of it before they take a test.

To continue with the hypothetical involving Prof. Lee, the next section contains profiles of three students from her class who will later appear when examining her implementation of differentiated instruction. In keeping with the fourth assumption, remember that any learning traits they display that seem to be tied to their cultural background and home life are not included as generalizations for all members of their cultural groups but are used here to show the possible intersection between their cultures and their learning styles.

In the final section of this chapter, critical information literacy will be used to examine the Association of College and Research Libraries' Framework for Information Literacy for Higher Education, its Information Literacy Competency Standards for Higher Education, and differentiated instruction as a tool to empower students to take control of their own learning.

HYPOTHETICAL: THREE STUDENTS

First Student: Henry

Henry is an 18-year-old student who plans to study nursing. His mother and aunt are both nurses, and he has wanted to follow in their footsteps since an early age. Both of Henry's parents are African-American and met working in the same hospital where they both still work, with his father serving as an x-ray technician. They also have another son and a daughter who are both younger than Henry. Many relatives of both parents live in the local area, and Henry spends several hours a week with his cousins and other relatives. Academically, Henry has always done well in his math and science classes but not as well in his other classes.

When Prof. Lee mentions in class that they will be using differentiated instruction in two sections later on in the course, Henry perks up and seems enthusiastic about it. He confirms this in his response to the second-to-last question on the preassessment and during their one-on-one meeting, where he tells Prof. Lee that some of his teachers in high school used differentiated instruction and that he liked getting to choose options that let him interact more with the material than just listening to a lecture and reading a textbook. He also felt that the teachers who differentiated their courses trusted him to take responsibility for his learning, which was a refreshing change compared to most of his teachers who he felt did not care about how students learned but only about doing things the way they have always been done. Prof. Lee is pleased to have such an enthusiastic student and to discover that differentiated instruction is an approach that some students are already familiar with and excited about.

Henry responds to the preassessment question about interests, "I plan to become a nurse. Some of my biggest interests are new developments in health care, science, state and local politics, and poetry." For the question about how he best learns, he writes:

> Some of my teachers in high school used differentiated instruction, and I liked it better than the usual way of teaching. I like working in groups on problem solving and projects. I get more out of watching a video than reading a textbook. I often make flowcharts when studying and like to study with other people around.

It comes as no surprise to Prof. Lee that Henry selects streaming videos, in-class group work, and in-class debates from possible learning objects choices given at the end of the questionnaire. He also chooses online practice quizzes. As best as Prof. Lee can tell based on Henry's own assessment of his learning preferences and her conversation with him, he seems to be a visual, kinesthetic, collaborative, dependent, and accommodating learner (prefers concrete experience and active experimentation).

Second Student: Janet

Janet is a 19-year-old who would like to be a software developer. Her interest in computer science stems from a middle school software coding class where all the skills taught seemed to come naturally to her. Her parents are both immigrants from Peru who arrived in the United States in their early twenties, 25 years ago, and who have now lived in the United States longer than they lived in their native country. All of their relatives remain in Peru, and they have few close friends. Janet has two older sisters, and the family has always been close-knit, spending most of their time together. Continuing to celebrate traditional Peruvian cultural customs has always been important to Janet's parents, who hope that their daughters will pass them on to their own children someday. The family visits Peru every three to four years to see relatives and to explore more of the country. Both parents learned English and earned their bachelor's degrees after coming to the United States and now work as paralegals at different law firms.

Janet has always gotten good grades in school, and a career assessment conducted by the guidance counselor at her high school showed a wide variety of different careers that she could expect to excel in. She mentions in her one-on-one meeting that she has never been in a class where the teacher has used differentiated instruction, and Prof. Lee gets a sense that Janet is a bit skeptical of the approach. She says she is concerned that straying from the traditional instruction she's used to could harm her chances of getting an A in the course because she knows that she always does well in traditionally taught classes.

Janet writes on her preassessment that, in addition to computer science, she is interested in consumer technology, video games, and cooking. In response to the question about how she learns best, she writes:

> Reading textbooks and taking notes while a teacher lectures in class have always worked well for me. I like to figure things out on my own and tend to study alone. I find condensing my notes into outlines and making flash cards helpful. I'd rather do individual projects than group projects.

She chooses the follow options from the list of different Content Delivery, Process, and Product choices given on the questionnaire: reading textbooks and articles, in-class lectures, podcast/audio lectures, online practice quizzes, and quick reflections written at the end of class.

From Janet's preassessment and Prof. Lee's observations, it seems that she is an aural, read-write, independent, and assimilating learner (prefers reflective observation and abstract conceptualization).

Third Student: Ken

Ken is a 20-year-old student who immigrated from Japan with his parents five years ago so that his father could teach political science at a local university. His mother has been a homemaker since his birth, soon after she completed college. Ken has been interested in becoming a pilot since the age of 13 and recently began taking private lessons. He decided to enroll in the community college's aviation program before moving on to a different school to earn a bachelor's degree and licensure as a commercial pilot. Ken is an only child and is accustomed to doing a lot of things on his own despite being part of a soccer team from his elementary school days through the end of high school, and he continues to play in an adult recreation league.

Ken has been an above-average student but never ranked near the top of his class. In addition to aviation and soccer, he shares on the preassessment that he is interested in documentary films and rock music. He writes that he learns best "by watching and listening to others explain things instead of having to do homework alone to figure it out. I take detailed notes and mostly study by reviewing my notes while pacing around my room." He told Prof. Lee that he's intrigued by the idea of differentiated instruction but is a bit hesitant because he thinks it may involve a lot of group work. He does not dislike group work but prefers learning directly from the teacher/instructor. The choices he made from the questionnaire's list reflect that preference: in-class lectures, streaming videos, in-class group work, individual activities, and online practice quizzes.

Between what Prof. Lee has been able to gather from Ken's preassessment, his meeting with her, and her observations of him in the first two classes, he seems to be a visual, aural, dependent, and diverging learner (preferring concrete experience and reflective observation).

EMPOWERING STUDENTS TO TAKE CONTROL OF THEIR LEARNING

In 2015, the Association of College and Research Libraries (ACRL) introduced its Framework for Information Literacy for Higher Education (Framework) to accompany its Information Literacy Competency Standards for Higher Education (Standards), which were adopted in 2000. The earlier Standards were criticized in the library and information science literature for being overly broad and mechanistic (Elmborg, 2006; Swanson, 2005; Tewell, 2015), for offering a single model of information literacy that is universally applicable to all individuals (Cope, 2010; Elmborg, 2006), for failing to address the need to think critically when engaging with information (Swanson, 2005), for reinforcing the outdated belief that some sources are "authoritative" without question (Cope, 2010; Hall, 2010; Kapitzke, 2001; Smith, 2013), for ignoring the politics and processes of knowledge production (Kapitzke, 2001; Seale, 2010), and for overlooking issues of social justice and social power (Cope, 2010; Elmborg, 2006). Much of this criticism raised concerns that are related to the central tenets of critical information literacy (Smith, 2013), and the creation of the Framework in part seemed to try to address some of these concerns.

Critical information literacy rejects a primarily skills-focused and generically universal view of information literacy, like that of the Standards, and instead emphasizes the importance of individuals becoming active agents in their learning by questioning the power structures present in the production and dissemination of information through critical reflection on the political, economic, and social frameworks surrounding information (Doherty & Ketchner, 2005; Dunaway, 2011; Elmborg, 2006; Luke & Kapitzke, 1999; Seale, 2010; Swanson, 2004; Tewell, 2015). Luke and Kapitzke (1999) suggest that critical information literacy should also consider "the development of local communities' and cultures' capacities to critique and construct knowledge" (p. 484).

The incorporation of critical information literacy concepts into instruction can help counter the problematic "banking concept" of education, where norms perpetuate a view that learners must passively accept and deposit information in their minds that educators and scholars determine is authoritative and valuable. The Standards reinforced this view by emphasizing the development of a set of skills dictated by educators as valuable for individuals to "recognize when information is needed and have the ability to locate, evaluate, and use effectively the needed information" (Association of

College and Research Libraries, 2000, quoting American Library Association, 1989). The banking concept of education was introduced by educational theorist Paolo Freire, whose work led to the development of a critical pedagogy approach to teaching that challenges repressive cultural and political forces preventing the empowerment of learners whose backgrounds do not align with those forces (Doherty & Ketchner, 2005; Elmborg, 2006; Elmborg, 2012; Smith, 2013; Swanson, 2004). Freire viewed knowledge not as neutral but rather as a reflection of dominant social, economic, and political views. Freire called on educators to aid students in developing "critical consciousness" by focusing on "problem-posing," where students seek to hone their ability to critically perceive the world around them, examine how that world influences the information and knowledge they encounter, and apply their own life experiences and cultural backgrounds to this critical analysis (Doherty, 2007; Elmborg, 2012; Hall, 2010; Swanson, 2004).

Critical information literacy seeks to address Freire's call by placing students at the center of the learning experience and empowering them to take control of their own learning. Given that students' unique sets of cultural background traits and personal life experiences influence how they view and interpret information, their perspective on the world around them differs from that of the instructor and their peers. Even for students whose backgrounds align with the white, straight, male, middle-class, Judeo-Christian, capitalist, American-born, Standard American English–speaking groups that have historically dominated knowledge making in the United States (Elmborg, 2006; Elmborg, 2012), their personal life experiences can alter their perspective. The cultural and political forces that limit some students who are from marginalized groups may not limit those students who belong to the dominant or mainstream groups that set the social, economic, and political agendas in our communities and our society. By guiding students in the practice of critically analyzing the sources of the information they are presented with or seek out in their education, academic instruction librarians can help students grow comfortable with the notion that information and knowledge should not be accepted as authoritative simply because a professor, librarian, scholar, author, publisher, or journal is the source. Students should be encouraged to critically evaluate the process of knowledge production and how information flows through that process, taking into consideration which groups have established the social, economic, and political views that have shaped the process and what the biases are of those groups' members. They should also be invited to lend their own personal perspectives and experiences to this inquiry, especially if they conflict with those of the groups that control the information creation process.

The Framework attempts to address some of the concerns of critical information literacy theorists in several of the six frames and their accompanying knowledge practices and dispositions, detailing more specific behaviors or actions that learners should be capable of demonstrating. The frame titled "Authority Is Constructed and Contextual" states:

> Information resources reflect their creators' expertise and credibility, and are evaluated based on the information need and the context in which the information will be used. Authority is constructed in that various communities may recognize different types of authority. It is contextual in that the information need may help to determine the level of authority required. (p. 4)

By acknowledging that various communities may recognize different types of authority, this frame addresses the concern that the Standards espouse a view that authority is universal, regardless of the community or communities one belongs to. However, some information scientists believe that this statement avoids conceding the reality that scholars, especially in academe, are the primary body dictating the dominant view of what information is authoritative through the lens of their community's norms (Foasberg, 2015; Rinne, 2017).

That reality is partially admitted in another frame, "Scholarship as Conversation," that states "Communities of scholars, researchers, or professionals engage in sustained discourse with new insights and discoveries occurring over time as a result of varied perspectives and interpretations" (p. 8). Although this claim does not specifically speak to who determines what information is authoritative, it somewhat weakens the impact of the Framework's earlier acknowledgment that communities may differ on the types of authority they recognize because it propagates an elitist position that those individuals in power in academic and professional settings decide how new knowledge and information should be interpreted. Despite the assertion that varied perspectives and interpretations are considered by those elites, the frame does not acknowledge the importance of giving nonelites a voice in how new knowledge is eventually interpreted.

The frame "Information Has Value" acknowledges that how information is interpreted and presented gives that information power when stating, "Information possesses several dimensions of value, including as a commodity, as a means of education, as a means to influence, and as a means of negotiating and understanding the world. Legal and socioeconomic interests influence information production and dissemination" (p. 6). Two of the knowledge practices associated with this frame directly addresses a concern of proponents of critical information literacy by putting forth the expectations that "[l]earners who are developing their information literate abilities understand how and why some individuals or groups of individuals may be underrepresented or systematically marginalized within the systems that produce and disseminate information; [and] recognize issues of access or lack of access to information sources" (p. 6) without suggesting that anything should be done to correct the power imbalance that comes from underrepresentation, marginalization, and lack of access.

Acknowledging the problematic aspects of information and knowledge creation, interpretation, dissemination, and access is a step in the right direction for addressing some of the blind spots of the Standards, but the ACRL leaves it up to information literacy instructors to address these problems, if at all, without much guidance within the Framework besides proscribing some related knowledge practices and dispositions that learners should be able to demonstrate or understand. A differentiated instruction approach to information literacy instruction, coupled with learning activities where students are invited to critically examine and reflect on the problematic issues surrounding information and knowledge, can help to address many of the concerns raised by critical information literacy theorists.

The student-centered design of differentiated instruction counters the banking concept of education by shifting the focus of learning away from passively receiving information from a central authority figure, the instructor, and placing the emphasis on students having agency throughout the learning process. Entrusting students with more responsibility in directing their learning by allowing them to choose learning objects empowers them to make decisions based on their learning styles and learning preferences, which are influenced by their cultures and life experiences. By giving students choice in how they engage with the material they are learning, differentiated instruction can help create a more comfortable learning space for students to critically question the power structures underlying the information and knowledge they seek. Students may be uncomfortable with the notion of questioning the authority of knowledge producers in an academic environment, especially when their background differs from the dominant groups, but they should be encouraged to do so openly and without any fear of repercussions.

Academic instruction librarians can help students develop critical consciousness by incorporating problem-posing learning activities in their courses, using examples that highlight how dominant social, economic, and political views influence what information and knowledge are deemed authoritative, as well as how the interpretation and dissemination of that information and knowledge can further the oppression of marginalized groups. Some topics to consider include the impact of government funding for academic and medical research on the creation of knowledge and information, barriers to information access, the influence of elite special interest groups, and how social justice issues that your students are concerned about are discussed by various press outlets, by government information sources, and in academic scholarship. Students should be encouraged to practice problem-posing through the filter of their own cultural and personal experiences. Using problem posing learning activities leads students to reflect not only on the role of the dominant forces that oppress affected groups but also on the way in which related information and knowledge can be constructed and disseminated to further their oppression. Academic instruction librarians can also reinforce to students that the information literacy knowledge and skills they will master in a course can be used throughout their lives to scrutinize the social, cultural, and political forces that drive information and knowledge creation and decide what information is deemed authoritative.

THREE

Preparing for Differentiated Instruction

The defining aspect of differentiated instruction is giving students choices in the Content, Process, and Product stages of learning so that they can select the option that best suits their level of readiness, their interests, and most especially their learning style. The process of implementing differentiation requires instructors to identify the most suitable units in the course for using the approach, to choose the design learning objects that appeal to different learning styles and interests, and to support students as they use those learning objects. This chapter guides you through the process of preparing for differentiation, followed by three chapters that present techniques and tools you can use when designing learning objects for each phase of differentiated instruction to make the adoption process easier.

One of the greatest benefits of differentiated instruction is that there is no expectation that every unit in a course must be differentiated. As the instructor, you have the flexibility to choose the topics or units you would like to differentiate and the ones you would like to continue to teach in a traditional manner. You may already know from prior teaching experience that certain topics are complicated and difficult for students to understand. It can be valuable to continue lecturing in the class sessions dedicated to those topics so that students can pose questions as they arise and seek clarification immediately. This flexibility allows you to test out how well differentiation works for you and your students on one or a few topics before deciding to differentiate the entire course. Testing out differentiation can also help you learn how much work is involved in the creation of new learning objects before you decide to differentiate multiple units or an entire course.

Whether you are differentiating one, several, or all of the units in a course, the success of differentiated instruction relies on creating clear objectives and learning outcomes before preparing any course content, synthesis tools, or assessments. This is especially important in the area of Product where rubrics must be created based on the learning outcomes in order to ensure fair grading of differentiated summative assessments that ordinarily come at the end of a unit or course. Determining clear learning outcomes first will make the process of creating Content, Process, and Product components easier because every learning object should be tied to at least one learning outcome.

BEGINNING WITH COURSE OBJECTIVES AND LEARNING OUTCOMES

The first step in preparing for differentiation, like the first step for any well thought-out instruction, is to create specific course objectives and learning outcomes. Course objectives map out what you will be teaching. Learning outcomes clearly describe everything that a student must master to successfully complete the course. Even if you are differentiating only one or a few topics, clear objectives will give your students a preview of what they are about to learn, while learning outcomes will help them determine whether they are on the path to developing the knowledge and mastery that you expect of them.

Course Objectives

Course objectives are broad or general statements about what will be taught in a course or unit and what students will be doing. These statements focus on the learning experience and provide students an overview of what they can expect to encounter in a unit. Giving students these expectations in advance can help them check from the outset whether they are taking in the big picture portions of what is contained in a unit. Course objectives should answer the question, "What will students do in a course or unit?" For example, in Prof. Lee's syllabus, the course objectives for the Critically Evaluating Sources unit are:

1. Students will evaluate information sources for accuracy, authority, objectivity, purpose, currency, and appropriateness.

2. Students will critically reflect on the political, economic, and social frameworks surrounding the production and dissemination of the sources.

Although each of the two course objectives contains a detailed description of what students do during the learning process, they do not provide any insight into what you as the instructor will be looking for in order to determine their mastery of the material, that is, what you will be grading students on. This comes later with the learning outcomes.

You may have noticed that each of the course objective statements begins with the words "Students will," followed by a verb that indicates some general learning activity, such as "evaluate" and "reflect" in this case. This is an effective structure for writing a course objective. Some of the verbs that often appear in course objectives are "learn," "understand," "appreciate," "think," "reflect," "know," "comprehend," "apply," "analyze," "synthesize," and "evaluate." If you are familiar with Bloom's Taxonomy of Educational Objectives, you will notice that the last six verbs reflect the six cognitive levels in the original version of the taxonomy.

Learning Outcomes

Learning outcomes are statements of the measurable or observable achievements that successful students will attain by the end of the learning process and then be able to demonstrate their mastery of in their final Products. Learning outcomes should be more detailed than course objectives because they describe the specific skills and knowledge that students are expected to develop during the unit or course. They should answer the question, "How will successful students show their mastery of the material?" and use verbs that are measurable or that describe something observable by you, the instructor, who will be assessing the students.

Prof. Lee designated the following learning outcomes for the first of the preceding two course objectives: "Students will evaluate information sources for accuracy, authority, objectivity, purpose, currency, and appropriateness":
Students should be able to:

• Determine the accuracy of an information source, describe their process for doing this, and justify their process and final determination convincingly.

- Examine the expertise and credibility of the author of an information source in the context of how the information will be used, determine whether the author's expertise and credibility are sufficient to lend authority to the source, describe their process for making this determination, and justify their process and final determination convincingly.

- Assess an information source's objectivity by identifying its facts, opinions, point of view, and bias; determine whether a source is sufficiently objective to be useful for its intended purpose; describe the process for making this determination; and justify their process and final determination convincingly.

- Determine the purpose for an information source and whether it is useful for the intended purpose, describe their process for making this determination, and justify their process and final determination convincingly.

- Determine whether a source is sufficiently current to be useful for its intended purpose, describe their process for making this determination, and justify their process and final determination convincingly.

- Assess whether an information source is appropriate for its intended purpose, describe their assessment process, and justify their process and final assessment convincingly.

These detailed learning outcomes provide students clear guidance on what skills development and knowledge acquisition they will be measured on at the end of the unit. The fact that these expectations are reinforced by each learning outcome, beginning with "Students should be able to," informs the students that Prof. Lee expects successful students to be able to demonstrate everything that is mentioned. The verbs used in learning outcomes should be more specific than the verbs used for course objectives. Verbs like "learn," understand," "appreciate," "think," and "know" should be avoided because they are too broad. If you are having difficulty finding the right verbs to use, remember that they should be measurable or should describe something observable. Prof. Lee has chosen the verbs "determine," "describe," "justify," "examine," and "assess" because she can observe whether a student has successfully demonstrated the skills needed to accomplish what follows each verb. All of the learning outcomes end with a statement like "describe their process for making this determination and justify their process and final determination convincingly" because Prof. Lee wants to communicate to students that they need not only to be able to demonstrate a skill through replication of what was done in class but also to be prepared to reason through why a certain process is effective.

Once you have clear and concise learning outcomes, you can more easily identify what should be conveyed by the Content learning objects. Every item of the material contained in Content should serve to get students started on the path toward eventually being able to achieve one or more of the learning outcomes. Similarly, every Process learning object should help students move from the initial step of interacting with Content to the final step of showing their mastery of one or more learning outcomes. Learning outcomes will also make creating rubrics for Products easier because rubrics should directly reflect what you are measuring or observing when grading students.

One common concern that instructors raise about using detailed learning outcomes is that they seem to reveal too much to students about what the instructor will be looking for when grading their Products. It is important to keep in mind that providing this level of detail at the beginning of a unit or course allows students to compare their skill development and knowledge acquisition against the learning outcomes at any time to ensure that they are making progress toward mastering what they are learning. Knowing exactly what they are expected to be able to demonstrate does not reduce students' responsibility in the learning process, but it does help prevent them from mistakenly focusing on things they are not expected to master.

PREASSESSMENT

Another important step in preparing for differentiated instruction is understanding your students' existing level of competency with information literacy and their professional and personal interests. You can use information about your students' interests to design learning objects that are more appealing to them by finding ways to incorporate their interests into examples and exercises. Even if you prepare all the differentiated learning objects you plan to use before the first day of class, administering a preassessment and questionnaire designed to determine students' readiness, to reveal their interests, and to investigate their learning styles may bring to light the need to adapt some learning objects to unexpected levels of readiness and incorporate some interests shared by many students.

In past courses, before learning about differentiation, Prof. Lee administered a preassessment to students to find out about their familiarity with the information literacy topics covered in the course and their past experience with developing relevant skills. Such a preassessment is necessary for determining students' level of readiness and can also be used to identify their interests. Although this book has mainly focused on learning style variations among students, differences in their readiness and interests can also be accommodated using differentiated instruction.

Readiness

Most college and university instructors are familiar with the practice of preassessing student readiness in math, science, or foreign language courses where students are given placement tests to determine their mastery of topics in those subjects in order to schedule them into the appropriate courses. Student readiness preassessments are often used in differentiated instruction in primary and secondary education to determine whether some students are able to begin working on material at a more advanced stage than some of their peers or whether some students need additional time with introductory material. It may seem that preassessing students' readiness may not be as fruitful a practice in a learning situation where all students will be encountering the same material at the same pace regardless of their existing knowledge on the subject, such as a college information literacy course. Although students may need to move through the material on the same timeline since all the units must be covered in the span of a semester, knowing each student's level of readiness is still valuable for differentiation. You may learn that many students have more knowledge of a particular topic than you expected and are able to modify the learning objects in the corresponding unit to reduce the amount of introductory material and start at a more advanced point. In order to accommodate students who are not familiar with the topic, you can make that introductory material available as a recommended resource. When planning for whole-group instruction, like a lecture, or for whole-group activities, such as an in-class discussion, knowing that some students are already familiar with a topic can give you confidence that they will have enough prior knowledge to speak up and participate early on in a unit, while other students are still making sense of what they are learning.

Having an idea of a student's prior knowledge can also help you divide students into groups when needed during differentiation. In some cases, you may want to group students who have a similar degree of readiness so that those who are already fairly familiar with a topic can work together to advance their understanding, while those students who are less familiar with a topic can be grouped together so that they can lend support to one another as they begin to develop their understanding. You can plan to dedicate more time to working with groups that are not familiar with a topic during an in-class activity to help get them to the level of understanding needed to succeed in the course.

Another approach you can take once you know students' level of readiness is to create mixed groups where some students are already familiar with a topic while others are less familiar. Mixing groups can lead to situations where the more familiar students help their less familiar peers raise their level of understanding. Mixed groups are especially useful in cases where less familiar students are having difficulty understanding what is explained in a textbook, lecture, or other Content. The more familiar students may be able to explain a topic using different terminology or offering examples that may be easier to understand for someone who is new to the topic. Consider using mixed groups in this way if you are not able to spend as much time as you might like working closely with each group.

Interests

Learning about your students' interests can help you when designing your Content, Process, and Product learning objects. Incorporating their interests into question prompts or activities may help students be more involved and attentive to the differentiated learning objects they are working on. For example, if you learn in a preassessment that many students have an interest in medical and allied medical careers and that several students are avid news readers, designing an in-class activity around a health- or medicine-related topic that has recently received heavy news coverage can result in more student enthusiasm for the activity. Rewriting an existing learning object to focus on a topic that students are interested in may require only a few minutes and pay off greatly when you see students eager to delve deeper into a topic.

Differentiating Process learning objects by interest is one of the primary ways you can incorporate critical information literacy problem-posing into your instruction. If you learn that many students are interested in a particular social justice issue, either through a preassessment or by observing their conversations in the classroom, you can design a Process learning object to examine the role of dominant social, economic, and political views in influencing the production and dissemination of information and knowledge about that issue. Students can look at the ways that the popular press, government information sources, and academic scholarship present that issue and how the views of members of the groups most affected by the issue are represented in those sources. Because social media plays a large role in disseminating information about social justice issues, you may also want to have students examine how the issue is framed in the social media by groups on both sides.

Learning Profiles

A preassessment is especially valuable for helping you decide which Content, Process, and Product learning objects to create for a course or unit based on students' learning profiles. Even if you have already created all the differentiated learning objects before the first day of class, a preassessment can still serve as a valuable tool in identifying areas where those learning objects may need modification. A preassessment may reveal that one of the learning objects is not as useful with a particular group of students because few of them have a learning style that a learning object was intended to accommodate, in which case that learning object can be left out for the current course and saved for future use. Because Prof. Lee decided before the start of the semester that she will be following a differentiated instruction approach in only two units that occur a few weeks into the course, she is able to wait until after the preassessment to decide which differentiated learning objects she will use from among those listed in the final question. Chapter Seven will follow Prof. Lee's process of choosing and preparing those learning objects.

Preparing a Preassessment

Identifying the goals of your preassessment will help you decide what format will best help you meet them. Do you want to assess student readiness by asking a question related to each topic in the course? Will asking questions about a few key topics be sufficient to assess readiness? Will using multiple-choice questions give you enough information about student readiness, or is it necessary to include short-answer questions? Do you want to learn only about students' professional interests or about their personal interests as well? For assessing learning styles, do you want students to choose from a list of learning traits or preferences or have them write about how they best learn? Do you want to include a list of different types of learning objects so that students can express their preferences, or would you rather determine the learning objects to use based on their answers about their learning traits or preferences?

Preassessments can take many forms. A questionnaire like the one Prof. Lee gives her students is one common approach to preassessment. Her questionnaire contains some of the statements from Rodney K. Marshall's Information Competency Assessment Instrument (http://works.bepress.com /rodney-marshall/4/), which contains 40 statements about information competency, such as, "I can confidently spot inaccuracy, errors, etc. in the information from mass media" and asks students to choose how strongly they agree or disagree with each on a seven-point Likert scale (Marshall, 2006). This type of self-assessment allows instructors to learn about what topics a student already feels competent with, but it does not reveal much about a student's actual skill level or prior knowledge.

Another common preassessment format that helps you learn more about students' skill levels is to use a quiz that includes questions similar to those they may see on a unit test or final exam. If you already administer quizzes in your course, you may want to make the preassessment questions easier than those you might give students after completing a unit. Some students may have enough familiarity with a topic to answer an easier question, and it is useful for your planning to find this out, but they may not be able to correctly answer a more difficult question. A preassessment quiz with only multiple-choice questions will probably take less time for students to complete, but including short-answer questions can give you a better sense of the extent of each student's familiarity with a topic. Of course, some students may not be very familiar with a topic but still guess the correct answer on a multiple-choice question. To avoid this, include "Do not know" as a choice for every question and encourage students to select that choice when they are not familiar with a topic rather than guessing at the other choices.

Many instructors who use preassessment quizzes administer the same quiz on the final day of class so that afterward students can compare their answers to those given on the first day and see the progress they have made toward mastering the skills and knowledge expected of them. This can provide students a confidence boost before taking on a final Product like an exam or project. If you plan to readminister the preassessment at the end of the course, consider including a question or two that students are less likely to be familiar with at the start of the course. Even if students are not able to answer these questions when they first take the preassessment, the questions provide students a preview of what they will be learning. Answering them correctly at the end of the course may provide that needed confidence boost. However, using formative assessments throughout the course is a more effective approach for student self-assessment of their progress and is recommended instead of administering the preassessment for a second time at the end of the course. More information about using formative assessment Product learning objects is provided in Chapter Six.

An additional approach that may work in a higher education information literacy setting is to pose a series of questions or scenarios related to information literacy skills and ask each student to write a few sentences in response to each. For example, "How would you go about determining whether a Web site is a credible source to rely on when writing a term paper?" or "What are the first few steps you take when given a research assignment?" These types of questions can reveal a student's knowledge, skills, and instincts if the responses are thoughtfully written.

Whether you use a questionnaire, quiz, or scenario-based preassessment instrument, it may be tempting to ask a large number of questions to ensure that every topic covered in the course is represented. This may be feasible but could end up being very time-consuming and taking up a large portion of your first class. In order to develop an instrument that is not excessively long, focus on including mostly questions on topics that you reasonably believe some students may already be familiar with. This allows you to learn whether some students are knowledgeable about a topic without occupying too much time with questions that the majority of students will not be able to answer. If you would like to administer a lengthy preassessment but do not want to dedicate a large portion of the first class to it, you can assign students the preassessment as homework. If your institution's learning management system includes a quiz tool, you can build the preassessment using that tool and add it to your course site. If a quiz tool is not available, you can create a free online quiz or submission form in Socrative, Google Docs, SurveyMonkey, or other similar software. Chapter Five contains more information about using these tools.

It is important to explain to students that you are administering a preassessment to determine whether some students are already familiar with one or more of the topics in the course and that you may adjust your lesson plans based on what you discover. You should let students know that the preassessment will not be graded or impact their performance in the course in any way. If you include questions about interests and learning styles and have not yet explained that you are planning to use differentiated instruction, you should do so when introducing the preassessment. As part of the explanation, you can provide a personal anecdote about your own familiarity or lack of familiarity with information literacy when you were at the stage in your education where they are now to help alleviate any anxiety students may have about not knowing enough going into the course. This also helps you build rapport with the class. Make sure your explanation for using differentiated instruction is student centered. This shows students that you are putting the effort into conducting a preassessment and differentiating in order to give them a more enriching learning experience that will hopefully pay off in their successfully mastering the material.

USING A FLIPPED CLASSROOM TO FACILITATE DIFFERENTIATION

A final consideration before beginning to design and create learning objects is whether you would like to adopt a flipped classroom instructional approach in conjunction with the differentiated units of your course. In a differentiated and flipped classroom, student engagement with Content learning objects takes place entirely outside the classroom setting, eliminating direction instruction, such as lectures. In its place, classroom time is dedicated to active learning using Process learning objects (Bergmann & Sams, 2012; Lage, Platt, & Treglia, 2000).

Adopting a flipped classroom is not necessary to successfully implementing differentiated instruction, but committing to a flipped approach can simplify your planning. Differentiation lends itself well to using a flipped classroom because, as you will see in the next chapter, nearly all of the options for Content learning objects can be delivered through a learning management system for students to engage with outside the classroom. Similarly, most of the Process learning object ideas presented in Chapter Five are intended to be used for in-class active learning. Many of the summative and formative assessment Product learning objects described in Chapter Six can also be administered via a learning management system or other online tool, making a flipped classroom instructional approach an ideal companion for differentiated instruction.

The primary goal of the flipped classroom is to maximize opportunities for active learning in the classroom (Hamdan, McKnight, McKnight, & Arfstrom, 2013). Because students engage with the substantive course material before coming to class, the entire class session can be dedicated to in-class activities and exercises, with students working alone or in groups under the supervision of the instructor. The role of the instructor changes from being the "sage on the stage" who offers direct instruction to becoming the "guide on the side" who works face-to-face with students on knowledge acquisition and skills development. Put into differentiated instruction terminology, Content is exclusively delivered and used outside the classroom, and in-class time is dedicated to students working with Process learning objects while receiving support from the instructor. Although there is no direct instruction in a flipped classroom, the first few minutes of the class can be reserved for the instructor to conduct a brief review of the information in the Content and to answer student questions before moving on to active learning exercises.

One common concern instructors raise about following a flipped classroom approach is that students may not complete the assigned Content work before class, resulting in their not understanding the material well enough to get the full benefit of the in-class Process learning objects (Aydin & Demirer, 2016; Bergmann & Sams, 2012). Flipped classroom adopters address this by requiring students to complete some form of online assignment before class to assess their understanding of the Content and show that they have done the expected work, such as a brief quiz or discussion board post (Papadopoulos & Roman, 2010; Zappe et al., 2009). Using this type of assignment to assess whether students are understanding the Content incorporates the Product phase of differentiation into the flipped classroom.

If you have already made the decision to eliminate direct instruction from the classroom as part of your planned differentiation in order to dedicate the majority of your face-to-face time with students to active learning, you have in effect decided to adopt a flipped classroom. As you read through the Content Delivery, Process, and Product techniques and tools presented in the next three chapters, ask yourself, "Will this work in a flipped classroom?" to help narrow down the options to consider. You will find that the majority of the items will work in a flipped classroom. Combining these two instructional approaches means that, for each unit, you should offer at least two options for how to engage with Content before class, give students a choice among multiple in-class Process learning objects, and offer some forms of assessment Products either before class or at the completion of a unit. If you intend to continue offering in-class lectures as part of your differentiated units, then a flipped classroom approach will not fit with your plans.

FOUR

Techniques and Tools for Differentiating Content Delivery

One of the most complicated aspects of differentiating Content is ensuring that the information conveyed to students is consistent among all of the learning object choices you give them. To begin differentiating Content, you first need to identify what essential information, ideas, and skills you need to teach your students. The course objectives you already identified should give you a good outline of the main topics and subtopics. Each Content learning object should start students on the path toward achieving one or more of the learning outcomes. If you are planning to offer a learning object that you do not believe is directly connected to any of the learning outcomes, you should consider excluding it because you do not want to ask students to learn about something that is not related to the material you expect them to master, unless you have a strong reason to still include it. Having a strong reason for including something not tied to a learning outcome may mean that your learning outcomes are incomplete and should be revised.

In traditional instruction, two Content learning objects are ordinarily used, lectures and reading assignments, but with differentiated instruction you can also make use of multiple additional Content learning objects. At times, you may believe that it is imperative that all students engage with a particular Content learning object, such as a reading assignment, because you want to be sure that they all get consistent information from that source. If so, you can certainly assign that reading to every student while offering them a choice among other additional Content learning objects.

The following sections contain descriptions of different approaches to Content Delivery, explanations of techniques that can be used for each approach, tips for implementation, and descriptions of different tools available for each technique. The explanation of each technique will also mention which learning styles or traits it accommodates, focused on the VARK and Grasha-Riechmann Learning Style Scales because many models contain some variants on these styles. Those specific learning styles are visual, aural, read-write, kinesthetic, avoidant, participative, collaborative, competitive, independent, and dependent, and they are summarized briefly in Figure 4.1.

The broad offering of suggested techniques and tools for differentiating Content presented in this chapter may give the impression that you will need to create a large number of Content choices in order to accommodate all of your students' learning style preferences. In reality, two or three Content choices can easily cover the learning needs of the nine styles and preferences listed in Figure 4.1. You may also find that it is cumbersome to accommodate some learning styles in this Content phase. There is no obligation to accommodate all nine of the learning styles focused on here. Content Delivery is the one area where it is especially difficult to differentiate for collaborative, competitive, and dependent students.

With the exception of an in-class lecture, all of the following Content ideas are meant for students to use outside the classroom, perhaps as part of a flipped classroom instructional approach. This will allow you to eliminate the need for a lecture and allocate that time for in-class Process experiences or exercises. If you would like to continue to offer an in-class lecture as one choice, keep in mind that some students will choose other Content options and that they will be working on Process or Product learning objects while you are delivering that lecture to the students who have chosen it. Those not participating in the lecture may find it distracting, and unless you are able to isolate those students somehow, you may need to eliminate lecturing when differentiating Content.

TRADITIONAL CONTENT DELIVERY

The use of techniques found in a traditional instructional approach should not be overlooked in planning for differentiation. Lectures and reading assignments accommodate aural, read-write, dependent, independent, and, potentially, visual learning styles. One benefit of traditional instruction is

VARKS Styles Learning

Visual

Learner prefers visual depictions of new information, such as graphics and diagrams.

Aural

Learner prefers auditory conveyance of new information, such as live or recorded speech.

Read-Write

Learner prefers receiving new information as text and showing mastery through written assessments.

Kinesthetic

Learner prefers to learn through experiences, by touching, moving, and participating in activities.

Avoidant

Learner shows no interest in learning. This learning style cannot be accommodated.

Participative

Learner enjoys learning and is fully involved in all learning activities.

Competitive

Learner is motivated by performing better than peers and becomes more stimulated when competing against peers.

Collaborative

Learner prefers to work with others to share ideas in group discussions and accomplish tasks through group projects.

Dependent

Learner shows little intellectual curiosity and relies on others for guidance about what to learn and how to learn it.

Independent

Learner is confident in abilities and prefers student-centered instructions where the learner can work alone.

Grasha-Riechmann Learning Styles

Figure 4.1 VARK and Grasha-Riechmann Learning Styles

that a multitude of resources and learning objects already exist for this dominant approach.

In-Class Lectures

Lecturing has many learning benefits and may be the right choice for Content Delivery in certain instances. Especially with topics that many students, including advanced students, struggle to grasp, lecturing may be your best option to ensure that students are not getting overly confused or misunderstanding the Content. Presenting new information in person allows students to interrupt you and ask for clarification the moment questions arise. It also permits you to stop and ask questions of the class for them to begin processing the Content or to make sure that everyone is following along. Lecturing accommodates students with aural and dependent learning styles. If you include graphics or other visual items as part of your lectures, such as a presentation slide deck that contains mostly images, this technique can also accommodate visual learners. Even if you decide only to lecture and not differentiate Content, you can still differentiate Process using in-class exercises if you set aside time for active learning by reducing the length of your lectures using some of the tips for condensing lecture material mentioned in the "Screencast Lectures and Mini-Lessons" section in this chapter.

Tips for In-Class Lectures

Design your lectures carefully to include only information that is essential for students to know. Remember that a lecture, like all Content, should set students on the path toward achieving one or more of the learning outcomes and that some students may stop following closely if they do not see a clear connection to what they are expected to master. Be sure to stop regularly to ask for questions or to pose questions to the class to have them begin processing the information instead of only passively absorbing the material.

Stylistic Options for In-Class Lectures

Consider using presentation slides, like PowerPoint, with many images to help accommodate students with a visual learning style. More information about how to do this follows in the "Presentation Slides" and "Graphics of All Kinds" sections. Presentation slides should contain minimal text because you do not want students to stop listening because they are distracted by the text. If you believe including a substantial amount of text is necessary, then you should consider giving an at-home reading assignment instead of lecturing.

Textbooks and Other Readings

Concise reading assignments are a valuable way to convey new information to students, especially those with read-write and independent learning styles. They can also be useful to students throughout their learning process because they can revisit the textbook or articles to clarify questions that may arise as they are learning.

Tips for Textbooks and Other Readings

Keep readings concise. If you are using a textbook and find that portions of a chapter are essential to what you are teaching but other portions may go beyond your students' needs, assign only the essential portions. If a textbook includes review or analysis questions at the end of a chapter, assign these so that students can begin making sense of what they are learning. You can also write your own review questions to accompany the reading and make these available to students via your institution's learning management system as a document or as a summative assessment Product, such as a review quiz (see Chapter Six for more on summative assessments).

Stylistic Options for Textbooks and Other Readings

Consider using an e-book version of a textbook or giving students the option to purchase one because many e-book readers contain text-to-speech functionality—it reads aloud to them—which can be helpful to auditory learners and visually impaired students. If you are assigning articles to read, try to make a screen-readable version available to students. Text on Web pages and Word or text documents are screen-readable. If you assign PDFs, check that the file contains screen-readable text and not just a scanned image of a printed page. You can do this by clicking anywhere on the page and, while still pressing down on the mouse button, dragging down to see if text is selected. If the PDF does not contain text, use the optical character recognition functionality available in most paid PDF software, such as Adobe Acrobat, which will add a screen-readable text overlay to the scanned image.

DELIVERY VIA MULTIMEDIA

Multimedia Content uses a combination of text, images, animations, audio, video, or interactive content to convey information. Multimedia can help accommodate a variety of learning styles depending on the types of media included in the mix. Text appeals to read-write learners, while images, animation, and video are preferred by visual learners. Audio, including animation and videos that contain audio, accommodate aural learning styles, while interactive content can be appealing to kinesthetic and active learners.

The complexity involved for an instructor incorporating multimedia in Content Delivery can vary from the simple inclusion of images found online to the creation of interactive learning tutorials for the more adventurous. Suggestions follow for a wide variety of techniques and tools to consider when differentiating Content with multimedia.

Presentation Slides

The multimedia format most commonly used in education is presentation slides, such as PowerPoint, Google Slides, or Prezi. Presentation software offers users the flexibility of including text, still images, animation, video clips, and audio clips. Preparing a presentation, often referred to as a slide deck, that conveys the new information for a unit and distributing it through your institution's learning management system can be as effective as sharing that information in a lecture, while freeing up in-class time for active learning Process activities and exercises. Presentation slides can also be incorporated into other Content learning objects, such as in-class lectures, recorded video lectures, or screencasts. Delivering Content using presentation slides accommodates the learning preferences of visual and independent learners.

Tips for Presentation Slides

Presentations can be as simple or complex as you feel comfortable making them. At a minimum, slide decks should contain mostly images, animations, videos, or audio that represent the concepts being explained and include only essential text, such as titles or headings and bullet points of the main takeaways. An exception to this is if the presentation is the sole Content learning object offered to students, in which case it is acceptable to include substantial text in lieu of a reading assignment or lecture-type content that will also appeal to students with read-write learning styles. Tips on selecting and using appropriate images, video, and audio are given in subsequent portions of the "Delivery via Multimedia" section.

Many instructors feel intimidated by the idea of creating a slide deck because they are concerned that they may not be very visually appealing. All presentation software contains a selection of template options that are colorful and offer different styles of slides. Some slide templates contain placeholders for text and a limited number of images or other visual media, while others contain multiple placeholders for visual media and no space for text. Find a template you like and explore the different types of slides contained within that template. If you use only the default slide format repeatedly, you may miss out on a layout that might better convey the information.

When adding images, video, and audio to a presentation that you will upload to a learning management system, be mindful of the file size because students will need to download the file from the learning management system to their computer or mobile device in order to view it, and they may have limited hard drive space or file storage available. You should also keep in mind that several students may look at the slide deck on a mobile device with a smaller screen, such as a smartphone or tablet. Images should be large enough to be identifiable on a smaller screen so that students know they will need to zoom in on the image to view the information being conveyed.

You should not feel restricted to choosing only templates that have a professional-looking design that might be appropriate for a presentation at a conference or in a boardroom. Choosing a template that contains a bit of visual flair or that uses flamboyantly bright colors can be entirely appropriate for learning content and may hold your students' attention more than something bland and corporate-looking. And do not hesitate to use different templates in different presentations throughout the course. Adding some variety in the templates you choose can make the process of creating presentations more interesting for you and viewing the presentations more interesting for your students too.

Recommended Software for Presentation Slides

Microsoft PowerPoint. PowerPoint is the best known presentation software and is available for purchase for Windows, macOS, iOS, and Android. A free Web browser version is also available with somewhat limited functionality. As of the publication of this book, all versions support adding text, images, tables, charts, shapes, and animations. PowerPoint contains a clip gallery with graphics that are licensed for use in presentations made in the software.

Video and audio can be added only in the Windows and macOS versions, although they can be played back in all versions. Embedding YouTube videos is supported only in the Windows version. Users with an Office 365 subscription can also record themselves narrating a presentation with the voiceover narration saved within the file. The narrated file can then be shared or exported as a video. PowerPoint has thousands of templates available to use.

Google Slides. This free, browser-based presentation application supports adding text, images, tables, charts, shapes, and videos to your slide deck. Hundreds of templates, called themes, are available. Because Google Slides is browser based, you can edit presentations anywhere you have an Internet connection and can share a link with students to view the presentation rather than having them download a file.

To add a video from a file stored on your computer, you will first need to upload it to Google Drive and then embed the file from the Google Drive location. Existing YouTube videos or videos you upload to YouTube are easy to embed.

Prezi. Another browser-based presentation application is Prezi, which supports adding text, images, tables, charts, shapes, audio, video, and animation. Prezi's layout is different from other presentation software because all of the content that would ordinarily appear on separate slides is organized as small items on a large canvas. The full canvas and the slide-like pages can be customized with one of hundreds of themes. When you first launch a Prezi, you see the full canvas, and as you progress through the pages, the screen zooms in on each page to display the content.

Prezi offers a free version that contains most features except that video files cannot be uploaded and inserted into your presentation, although YouTube videos can be embedded. The free version does not offer shareable links but can be used in an in-person presentation or a screencast. In order to share a Prezi link with students to view on their own devices, you need a paid plan with an educational discount. The paid plan supports video uploads.

Apple Keynote. This free presentation application is available for macOS and iOS, along with a browser-based version that also supports Windows. Keynote features include the ability to add text, images, tables, charts, shapes, audio, video, and animation. It also offers voiceover narration similar to that offered in PowerPoint, but the narrated slides cannot be exported as a video.

Graphics of All Kinds

Using graphics such as images, comics, diagrams, pictographs, info-graphics, and graphic organizers in your Content is a creative and cognitively impactful way to engage students and to convey data, information, and knowledge visually. "Data," "information," and "knowledge" are not synonymous terms, and it is worth clarifying the differences because they appear frequently in this section. *Data* are simple facts presented without any interpretation to give contextual meaning. *Information* conveys meaning through the contextual interpretation of facts. *Knowledge* lends insight to information based on experiences or education. When speaking generally about graphics, the term "information" is used in this section, and the other terms appear only when it is necessary to distinguish among the three.

Although you cannot convey all of the information being taught through graphics alone, they can help visual students create an association between the information and the image that will make a more lasting impression on them and help them recall it later on. Graphics can also make Content learning objects more engaging for all students, compared to sharing information through text alone. The process of viewing an image or other graphic and making an association between it and the new information is a more active experience for students than passively reading text or transcribing the main points of a lecture into their written notes. Images and other visual means to share information may not feel as formal or scholarly as other means of delivering Content in higher education, but claiming adherence to formality as an excuse for not using graphics comes at the expense of not giving students an additional avenue to help them learn and retain information.

One of the greatest concerns instructors have about using graphics in their courses is whether they can be liable for copyright infringement if they use copyrighted material. Because the vast majority of graphics one comes across online are copyrighted, it is important to understand the copyright implications of using graphics before delving into the various related techniques and tools.

Copyright Concerns for Using Graphics

With most of the categories of graphics mentioned in this section, you will be able to find plenty of usable or modifiable items within software image galleries, clip art galleries, and online. There is no need to be concerned about copyright infringement when using software image galleries and clip art galleries because the graphics have been licensed for use in documents and presentations prepared in those applications. However, you need to be careful when using the graphics you find online, including those from some of the sources suggested in the resources sections for each of the following categories.

If you are looking for graphics online, one best practice is to look for public domain images where copyright protection has expired or has been entirely waived by the creator. Several of the sites compiled in the "Recommended Resources for Still Images" section in this chapter allow you to search for public domain graphics, which will be noted in their descriptions. When possible, you should attribute the public domain work as a courtesy to the original creator, although this is not required because the work does not have any copyright protection.

Another best practice is to search for items that are available under a Creative Commons license. Creative Commons is a public copyright licensing scheme where the creator has designated the graphic or other creative work for free public use. Sometimes Creative Commons licenses come with certain stipulations, such as not allowing the work to be used commercially or not granting permission for others to create derivative works by modifying or transforming the original work. If you use a graphic distributed under a Creative Commons license, be sure to always give attribution to the original creator. More information about Creative Commons can be found on the organization's Web site (https://creativecommons.org), which also includes a search engine for images and other creative works licensed for public use (https://search.creativecommons.org).

If a graphic is not in the public domain or licensed under Creative Commons, the safest approach is to seek permission from the creator to use that graphic. Many creators of original digital content that you find openly available on the Web are more than happy to grant permission for educational use of their work. The Contact or About page on most Web sites will provide contact information for a webmaster or author. If you find a graphic you would like to use but do not believe that the author of that page is its creator, you can save that image file to your computer and then run a Google Images search (https://images.google.com) for other instances of that graphic to help determine the original creator. To search by image using that file, click on the camera icon that appears on the right portion of the search bar. You can also paste in the URL to an image in a Google Images search, but be sure that the URL points directly to the image and not to a page containing the image.

U.S. copyright law includes a Classroom Use Exception that permits educators at nonprofit institutions to display or perform any copyrighted work without first seeking permission but only in an in-person, classroom setting. Under the Classroom Use Exception, you can display any graphic you would like in the classroom or as part of a slide deck at a nonprofit institution. However, if you make that graphic available on your learning management system for students to view or download, either on its own or as part of a slide deck or other multimedia content item, the Classroom Use Exception does not apply.

Most academic instruction librarians have some familiarity with the legal doctrine of fair use, which is not an exception to copyright law but rather a provision in the law that allows for unlicensed use in certain circumstances. The determination of whether a graphic or other copyrighted work can be used without permission under fair use is made on a case-by-case basis. The legal provision includes four factors that must be weighed together when determining whether fair use applies. The only government body that can make a determination of whether the unlicensed use of a work is fair use is a federal court. Because of this, anyone seeking to make fair use of a creative work will need to examine their intended use under the four factors and make their own determination of whether it is likely to be fair use. The U.S. Copyright Office's Circular 21, Reproduction of Copyrighted Works by Educators and Librarians, provides helpful guidance. The Visual Resources Association's "Statement on the Fair Use of Images for Teaching, Research, and Study" is also a helpful resource when assessing whether you are likely making fair use of a graphic.

The four fair use factors under federal statute 17 U.S.C. § 107 are:

1. *Purpose and character of the use, including whether the use is of a commercial nature or is for nonprofit educational purposes:* Courts considering a fair use argument are more likely to find that nonprofit

educational uses are fair. This is not blanket permission for all non-profit educational use, but this will be weighed in consideration with the other factors. "Transformative" educational uses that modify the work and add something new to it in order to serve a different purpose than the original work intended will more likely be found to be fair use.

2. *Nature of the copyrighted work:* Unlicensed use of works that are highly creative, such as fiction writing or paintings, are less likely to be seen as fair use than unlicensed use of mostly factual works, like a news article. Using unpublished works without permission are also less likely to be considered fair than published works.

3. *Amount and substantiality of the portion used in relation to the copyrighted work as a whole:* This factor weighs the quality and quantity of the work that was used. The greater the portion of a work that is used, the less likely the use will be considered fair. As for substantiality, if some portions of a work are less creatively important than others, using those more important portions are less likely to be considered fair use. Using a stage play script as an example, dialogue occurring at the climax of the play is more creatively important than stage directions stating that a minor character walks onto the stage early on in the script.

4. *Effect of the use upon the potential market for or value of the copyrighted work:* This factor looks at the economic impact the use has on the market for the work. For example, distributing a substantial portion of a work to students to avoid them having to purchase a copy reduces the number of sales of that work and has a detrimental impact on the market for it. This distribution would most likely count against a claim of fair use when weighing this factor among the others.

If you decide, after examining your intended use in light of these four factors, that it is a fair use, you may want to make a note to yourself explaining why you came to this decision, although this is not required. There is no need to notify anyone that you are planning to make what you believe is a fair use of a creative work.

Still Images

Including still images, such as photos, in your Content, can provide real-world context to what is being taught. For example, rather than just telling students that authors and other creators can have political, social, and economic bias that color the way they present information, you can use a slide that has the word "Bias" as the title and that otherwise shows only images of a political rally or protest, people from non-Western societies, and piles of money or other symbols of opulence. Although these images do not in any way represent the full aspect of how authors can have biases, a single visual representation for each type is enough context for students to understand that bias is not an amorphous concept but is rooted in the real-life experiences and perspectives of the author. Students' imaginations may even reinforce the point being conveyed by making up a quick story in their minds that connects the concept to the image. Seeing an image of a political protest may trigger a student's imagination to come up with a story in a second or two of a politically involved person attending the protest and going home to write a bias-heavy blog post. That type of cognitive connection can be more impactful for a student than reading text on a page that authors can have political bias.

Tips for Still Images. The images you choose do not have to have an obvious, direct connection to the concept or idea but should be sufficiently related for your students to be able to make that connection on their own. If the connection is a bit attenuated, be sure to explain to your students the significance of that image. When organizing multiple subtopics on a single page, consider using images in place of headings for each of those subtopics. If you are revising an existing slide presentation to incorporate more images, look for areas that contain extensive text and try to locate an image that can replace the text by depicting a scene that is similar.

Recommended Resources for Still Images. A number of Web sites let you search for public domain and Creative Commons–licensed images that you can use freely, with attribution, in addition to the Creative Commons Search capability already mentioned. Google Images contains an advanced search feature that allows you to filter your search results to show only those that are labeled for noncommercial use. To do this, first run a search and then choose Settings, Advanced Search, and from the bottom of the advanced search screen, select the usage rights option for images that are free to use or share. Bing's image search (http://www.bing.com/images/) similarly offers a filter to limit its results to those that are freely usable by first running a search, clicking the Filter option, and then, from the License menu, choosing the option for images that are free to use or share.

Wikimedia Commons (https://commons.wikimedia.org) is a collection of user-contributed images and other media that can be freely used. Everystockphoto.com, Pixabay (https://www.pixabay.com), Pexels (https://www

.pexels.com), Unsplash (https://unsplash.com), and FreePhotos.cc (https://freephotos.cc/) also allow you to search for freely usable images. StockJo (https://www.stockjo.com) goes beyond searching for free images and also enables you to search for free graphics of other kinds, such as videos, audio, fonts, vectors, software, and other resources.

If you have funds available to purchase licensed images, Shutterstock (https://www.shutterstock.com), iStock by Getty Images (https://www.istockphoto.com), 123RF (https://www.123rf.com), and Adobe Stock (https://stock.adobe.com) all offer large collections of images that can be either purchased individually for licensed use or downloaded with a subscription that allows you to access a certain number of high-resolution images each month.

Comics, Cartoons, and Memes

Comics, cartoons, and image-based memes offer another visual vehicle for students to make associations between a concept and real-world experiences. Comic strips, political cartoons, comic books, graphic novels, and online comics can reinforce what is being taught and provide context by telling a memorable story with one or a few images. Using image-based memes can both entertain students and convey an idea by using humor while drawing on their familiarity with the meme. Suggestions for meme generators that let you customize the image with your own text follow in "Recommended Resources for Comics, Cartoons, and Memes."

Tips for Comics, Cartoons, and Memes. These graphics can have visual elements you would like to use but the text in a speech bubble may not be relevant. A simple way to replace the text is to open that image in one of the presentation software tools previously mentioned and place a text box over the speech bubble, allowing you to type in whatever text you would like. You can then either export that image or take a screenshot of it and use the modified image in your Content.

Recommended Resources for Comics, Cartoons, and Memes. Many popular comic strips and political cartoons are available on GoComics (http://www.gocomics.com) and azcentral (http://comics.azcentral.com).

Meme generators allow you to customize popular image-based memes by adding your own text. Meme Generator (https://memegenerator.net), Imgflip (https://imgflip.com), and Make a Meme (https://makeameme.org) all contain many popular memes. Most images that serve as a basis for memes are copyrighted, but the superimposing of ordinarily humorous text on these images creates a transformative work, and this consideration should be factored into your fair use analysis.

Diagrams, Charts, and Tables

Diagrams and other visual tools that organize closely related information or data, such as charts and tables, give students a visual reference point for how to cognitively group pieces of information together and find relationships between and among them. Paragraph after paragraph of text may cause concepts to blur together for students who can get lost within a large amount of dense, new information. Organizing ideas, concepts, and data that are closely related can clarify the associations among items. Diagrams show relationships between and among related information, displayed in such common formats as flowcharts, decision trees, and organizational maps. Charts are used to convey data visually, while tables display data in rows and columns.

Tips for Diagrams, Charts, and Tables. You may be able to find diagrams, charts, and tables in existing teaching resources and materials that other academic instruction librarians make available online. However, this is one area where you may find yourself having to create original Content. If you do not feel comfortable with using any of the software tools mentioned in the "Recommended Resources for Diagrams, Charts, and Tables" section, consider hand-drawing a diagram or chart and scanning it into an image. Do not be concerned about it not looking as professional or polished as something created in software. What is most important is conveying the information to your students.

Even if you do not create your own diagrams, charts, and tables, suggest to students that they create them as part of their process of making sense of what they are learning because some students may have never considered doing this, and it can be especially beneficial for visual learners. Your students can also be a great source for charts and similar items. After completing a unit or at the end of the course, ask whether they have created their own charts or diagrams as part of their notes or study material and whether they would be willing to share them with you to use in future courses.

Recommended Resources for Diagrams, Charts, Tables. Word processing and spreadsheet software applications ordinarily include features for table and chart creation, and some may contain diagramming functionality. Microsoft Word, Microsoft Excel, Google Docs, Google Sheets, Apple Pages, and Apple Numbers all allow you to create tables and charts to visually display data. Microsoft Word, Google Docs, and Apple Pages also support creating diagrams to organize information.

A number of online services provide free browser-based diagram, infographic, and graphic organizer design tools with hundreds of templates available, although some templates are available only to their paid subscribers. Venngage (https://venngage.com) and Canva (https://www.canva.com) offer free access with limited functionality that allow you to test out their editors, but your graphic cannot be downloaded unless you subscribe to a paid plan with an educational discount. Infogram (https://infogram.com) similarly does not let you download your graphic without an education subscription, although after you have designed a graphic, you can take advantage of a free trial that does allow downloading. Visme (https://www.visme.co) permits downloading with their free account. Piktochart (https://piktochart.com) also allows downloading of graphics you create with a free account and offers the least expensive educational subscription.

Pictographs

Pictographs are images in which a symbol or grouping of symbols stand in for a physical object, concept, or other piece of information. Street signs or signage in airports make heavy use of pictographs. Using symbols can have an effect similar to that of still images for making real-world associations in students' minds. Returning to the earlier examples of images used to convey types of bias in authors, using clip art of a checklist to represent a ballot and thus political bias, a globe or world map to represent social bias, and a dollar sign to represent economic bias can reinforce these concepts for students.

Recommended Resources for Pictographs. There are many free or already licensed options for finding pictographs to use in your multimedia Content. Clip art galleries in your presentation and word processing software contain icons and other pictographs licensed for your use. Many Web sites also offer large collections of icons that are available under Creative Commons licenses. Flaticon (https://www.flaticon.com) contains the largest collection of free icons usable with attribution. The Noun Project (https://thenounproject.com) is a popular resource for educators that contains thousands of black-and-white icons. Although Iconfinder is a paid service, it does offer a free area (https://www.iconfinder.com/free_icons) with thousands of color and black-and-white icons.

Emojis are a popular type of pictograph that can now be easily added alongside text on Windows PCs, Macs, and Chromebooks. This standardized set of expressive faces, objects, places, weather symbols, and animals contains hundreds of pictographs. Emojis may appear slightly different on each operating system because the emojis are Unicode characters, similar to the alphanumeric characters on a keyboard, and each operating system uses its own visual set of pictograph symbols for the emoji characters, similar to how an alphanumeric character looks slightly different from one font to another. Since an operating system's set of emojis are more or less equivalent to a font, you do not need to be concerned about copyright infringement when using emojis because they will be displayed to viewers in the format that is licensed for the device they are using.

If your Windows PC has been updated since late October 2017, an emoji picker is built in. To access it, press the Windows key and Period key together, and it will appear. On a Mac, press and hold down the Command and Control keys while pressing the Spacebar to see the emoji picker.

Enabling access to the emoji picker on a Chromebook requires making a change in the settings rather than pressing a specific key combination, but once it is enabled, it will be easily accessible from that point forward from the shelf at the bottom of the screen. To access Settings, click on the area in the far right of the shelf where the time appears, and click on the gear icon in the menu that pops up. Scroll down to the bottom of the Settings screen and click the "Show advanced settings" option. From there, scroll down to the "Language and input settings . . ." button which will activate a pop-up window. In the lower portion of the window check off the box next to "Show input options in the shelf." A button will now appear on the shelf that will reflect the type of keyboard you are using. For example, the button will display "US" for the U.S. QWERTY keyboard. Clicking that button will make a menu appear that shows all the enabled input methods, including a smiling face emoji along the bottom that will open the emoji picker when clicked.

Infographics

Infographics can be used to present several related ideas by combining both text and visual elements to convey a mix of data, information, and knowledge. Figure 4.1 (page 47) is an example of an infographic. They are especially useful when showing the relationship between ideas that occur on several levels. For example, using a pyramid with different layers as part of an infographic can cue the viewer that the idea represented by the bottom-most, widest tier of the pyramid is the broadest or most cognitively simple of the various ideas, while the idea at the top is the narrowest concept or most cognitively complex. Infographics can also provide summaries of information that combine the learning benefits of images, charts, and pictographs into one visual display.

Tips for Infographics. You can find a large offering of infographics online that may be usable or modifiable to suit the topics in your course. If you need to create your own infographics, do not hesitate to use simple shapes, lines, and arrows to design them within your word processing software. As with charts and diagrams, you can always hand-draw an infographic and scan it to make it an image file.

Recommended Resources for Infographics. You can create infographics in Microsoft Word, Google Docs, and Apple Pages using the built-in diagram tools. The online tools Venngage, Canva, Infogram, Visme, and Piktochart also support creating infographics.

Graphic Organizers

Graphic organizers, also known as mind maps, knowledge maps, or concept maps, are teaching and learning diagrams that, like infographics, use a mix of visual symbols and text to convey ideas and relationships between them. Graphic organizers are valuable for showing the relationships between a large number of ideas that would otherwise be crowded together if conveyed in an infographic. One popular approach is to visually organize ideas as spokes on a wheel, with one or a few large circles used for the main topics and smaller circles coming off those to represent subtopics. Lines and arrows can be drawn between circles to show the relationships between ideas.

Using graphic organizers for Content Delivery can be useful at the start of a unit to provide a roadmap for what topics and subtopics will be covered and how they relate to one another. At the end of the unit, they can offer a succinct visual summary of everything that was taught. You can also encourage students who are visual learners to create their own graphic organizers as part of their Process of making sense of what they learn.

Tips for Graphic Organizers. Hand-drawing a draft of a mind map or a graphic organizer may be the best way to start. Quickly sketching out how you would like to organize information into larger topics and smaller subtopics can help you visualize how you would like the information to be organized ultimately. Once you have a loosely created map, you can then use one of the online or software tools listed in the next section to build out your full graphic organizer.

Recommended Resources for Graphic Organizers. Graphic organizer templates are available in Venngage, Canva, Infogram, Visme, and Piktochart. A number of free online tools also exist for the creation and downloading of mind maps. Coggle (https://coggle.it) and MindMup (https://www.mindmup.com) are two popular, easy-to-use options. Bubbl.us (https://bubbl.us) does not require you to create an account to create and download a graphic organizer, although one is needed to save your mind map. Downloadable, free, open-source options also exist, such as Freemind (http://freemind.sourceforge.net) and Freeplane (https://www.freeplane.org). Paid, downloadable software options also exist, such as XMind (https://www.xmind.net) and Mindomo (https://www.mindomo.com).

Recordings of In-Class Lectures

Video recording yourself delivering a lecture in a classroom and afterward making it available to students is another way of differentiating Content. This lecture can be delivered either in an empty classroom or in front of a class full of your current students for use in future courses. You can then deliver this content to students as a downloadable video or as a streaming video. Taking this approach allows you to still deliver all of the lecture content you would ordinarily give in traditional instruction while freeing up in-class time. Like a traditional lecture, this approach appeals to visual and independent learners.

Tips for Recordings of In-Class Lectures

If you record a lecture that you are delivering to a classroom of students, check with your school's audiovisual, media, or educational technology department to see whether the enrollment agreement students sign contains a provision granting permission for them to be recorded for instructional purposes. If not, you may need to have students sign waivers before recording. Because classroom recording is a common occurrence, the appropriate department should already be familiar with this request.

Your institution may have a lecture capture system with certain classrooms already equipped with cameras and microphones to record lectures. If you are not sure, check with the appropriate department. If your institution does not have lecture capture, the camera you use should be placed in a position where you and any projection screen or board behind you are clearly visible.

It is important to test out the sound and video quality before recording a full lecture. It is preferable to use a microphone so that you can record clear audio rather than projecting loudly for the camera microphone to capture your voice from a distance. Any notes that you write on a board or images you project on a screen, such as presentation slides, should be clearly visible in the video. Many learning management systems support video uploads and will make the video available at either the original quality or as a high-quality compressed file. If your institution has its own streaming media server and you plan to request that the video be uploaded there, ask that the video file remain at a high quality so that all images and notes behind you are visible. Videos uploaded to YouTube will be available at the original quality, but on a slow Internet connection, the quality may automatically be lowered to prevent viewers from having to wait a long while for the video to stream.

Screencast Lectures and Mini-Lessons

Screencasting is a popular Content creation technique where screen capture software records what is happening on a computer screen and can also capture the internal computer audio or microphone audio. Screencasting in education often involves using presentation slides containing lecture-like content that are displayed on the screen while the instructor narrates as they would during a lecture, accommodating the learning preferences of aural, visual, and independent learners. Any video where a narrator is speaking while multimedia content appears on the screen is a screencast, such as Khan Academy videos or many online video advertisements without actors. Students tend to like the option of viewing screencasts in place of an in-class lecture because they can pause a video to take notes, replay a portion they may not fully understand, and rewatch the videos later in the semester to review or prepare for a final Product.

Although screencasting can most obviously serve as a substitute for lectures in order to free up in-class time for active learning, it can also be used to create short tutorials for using online research databases and other electronic resources. Because screencasting software captures whatever is visible on a computer screen or on a preselected region of the screen, tutorial videos can show how an electronic resource is used while the narrator explains features and the steps of using the resource.

If you plan to use screencasts to replace your lectures, consider breaking down your lecture content into several mini-lessons. Research has shown that attention spans continue to shrink (McSpadden, 2015) and offering several mini-lessons in place of one lengthy lecture allows students to view a portion of the content and return later to view the remaining mini-lessons.

Tips for Screencast Lectures and Mini-Lessons

Write a script for what you are going to say before recording a screencast. Regardless of how experienced you are with delivering a lecture on the topic, it is helpful to have at least a very detailed outline of what you plan to say before you start recording. This helps avoid excessively long pauses that you will later need to edit out and will reduce the number of times you stumble over your words. Your screencast does not need to be perfect, but taking the time to write a script will help with your delivery of the narration. Practicing your script at least once before recording can reveal topics where a particular point needs further explanation or additional visual content and can also make you feel more at ease before beginning. A script is also an incredibly valuable resource if you are planning to add closed captioning to your video because all of your narrated text already appears there, except for any portions you ad lib.

If you are going to use existing lecture notes as the basis for a screencast or series of mini-lessons, consider first scrutinizing those notes and deciding whether every piece of information that you included in the lecture is essential to the screencast. Your lecture notes may have been written in order to provide sufficient information to fill a class period, but there is no requirement for a screencast or series of screencasts to be as long as a class period. Careful examination and distillation of existing lecture notes into only essential information can reduce the amount of time for your screencasts by one-half or more. Videos should be no longer than 15 minutes, but breaking up a long lecture's worth of content into several mini-lessons that are much shorter than 15 minutes can be more effective for your students.

You will most likely be creating a screencast in an office or studio where you are alone, and it may feel awkward to be speaking to an empty room. Inviting a colleague, student, or friend to sit in with you while you record to serve as an audience may help reduce this feeling of awkwardness. If you are ordinarily standing when you deliver an in-class lecture, gesture regularly when you speak, and pace back and forth while in front of a classroom, you may want to do all of these things while recording your screencast. This will help you feel more comfortable and relaxed, and your voice will probably sound more natural to the listener. If you do plan to pace while you narrate, be sure to use a headset with a microphone because otherwise you will be moving away from and back to a stationary microphone, and your volume level will shift as you pace.

Delivering your screencast as a streaming video is preferred over making it only available for download from a learning management system because streaming videos do not occupy hard drive storage space on students' devices. It is easy to create a YouTube channel and upload your videos there. One benefit of YouTube is that videos can be streamed on any computer or mobile device. During the upload process, you can set the permissions for your video to be unlisted so that they will not appear in the search results on YouTube or on Web search engines if you would like to limit the viewers to only individuals who have a link to the video, like your students. However, that link can be shared by students with anyone they choose. A more restrictive setting is to make videos private so that they are viewable only to the YouTube accounts you share the video with. You need to add each account's e-mail address to a list of accounts permitted to view the video. This can be a tedious additional step if you are uploading several videos because this needs to be done for each video.

Your learning management system likely offers students the option of watching videos that you upload as streaming videos rather than only permitting them to be downloaded, but that feature may not be fully functional on mobile devices, which may be some students' preferred way of watching videos for their courses. Your institution may also subscribe to a video streaming service other than YouTube or have its own video server that supports streaming. Check with your audiovisual, media, or educational technology department.

One important tool for screencasting is a microphone. Your institution's audiovisual, media, or educational technology department may be able to lend you a USB microphone that connects to your computer. If you would like to purchase one, several popular USB microphones are reviewed briefly in the "Recommended Resources for Screencasting" section. If you have a smartphone that came with earbuds with an in-line microphone, you can also use that microphone to record the narration for a screencast on your computer, although the quality will likely not be as good as with a USB microphone. With any of these options, check the sound or audio settings on your computer to make sure that the input source is your microphone. Make sure to keep your mouth the same distance from the microphone while narrating. Otherwise, the narration will sound louder or quieter as you move closer to or away from the microphone. If you use a desktop microphone, you may want to place a few books underneath it so that it is at about the same height as your mouth. A common way to measure the distance between your mouth and the microphone so that you will sound clear when speaking at your normal volume is to make two fists with your hands, put them end to end so that the thumb side of one fist is resting against the pinky side of the other, and place them between your mouth and the microphone.

You will need to record in a quiet space where sounds do not echo in order to achieve the best narration sound quality. Make some test recordings in the place you plan to record to check for echoes or background sounds, like chatter outside your office door or street noise. Close out of all other software applications before beginning to record in order to avoid any notification sounds from interrupting your recording. This also frees up more of your computer's processing power and can ensure that your screencasting application will run smoothly.

If you take the approach of displaying presentation slides on the computer screen while you are narrating the slides, then you should include only minimal text on those slides. The substance of what you are conveying should be included in the narration. You should include closed captioning if you have hearing-impaired students in your course. Also be aware that your institution's universal design policy may require that you include closed captioning regardless of whether you have any hearing-impaired students in your course.

Remember that some students will be viewing the screencast on a small screen on a mobile device, so all images should be large enough where they can be clearly visible on small screens. If you are creating a tutorial, such as an introduction to an electronic resource, zoom in on your browser so that the text and features visible on the screen are larger than you usually display them when working in that resource and they are easier for the viewer to see. In most screencasting software, you can select only a portion of your screen to record, such as a browser window or another application's window, which is especially useful in creating tutorials where you may not be demonstrating a resource in full-screen mode.

Two concerns screencast creators frequently raise are that they are uncomfortable listening to the sound of their own voice when playing back a recording during the editing process and that they find editing to be very time-consuming. Keep in mind that although you are not accustomed to hearing your own voice in that manner, that is the voice your students hear in class. If you create many screencasts, with time you will grow more comfortable with listening to your own voice. As for the editing process, it can be tempting to cut out every extra word or long pause, but keep in mind that all of these things happen when you deliver a lecture live in class, and students don't expect a screencast to have perfect, professional production value. Students regularly watch streaming videos online that are made by nonprofessional users and are accustomed to viewing videos that are not heavily edited.

Most screencasting software allows you to pause in the middle of a recording. This feature is convenient if you need a moment to take a sip of water or collect your thoughts before continuing on with your screencast. If the screencasting software you choose does not have a pause button, you will need to use a video editor to cut out any long stretches of silence in the recording.

During the recording process, you may make a narration mistake that you would like to edit out later. When this occurs, snapping your fingers close to the microphone or making some other loud sound close to it will mark that point in time for you to edit later. When you are finished recording, you can either listen for that sound to alert you to edit out the preceding portion or, if your screencasting software displays the audio waveform of the narration, you can look for large spikes in the waveform and listen to the preceding portion to determine what you need to delete.

Because students will not be able to interrupt you to ask a question while they are watching a screencast, make sure they know you are available to answer questions via e-mail or during office hours. An alternative is to create discussion posts in your institution's learning management system for each of the screencasts so that students can asks questions and everyone in the class can see your answers in the event they have the same question.

Recommended Software for Screencasting

There are over 30 screencasting software options for Windows, a similar number for macOS, and several for iOS and Android mobile operating systems. The following nine recommended software applications cover the range of these operating systems and include free and paid options. Use

Table 4.1 to help you decide which options are best suited for your situation before reading the following descriptions. (*Note:* All prices in the following sections were valid at the time of writing this book.)

ActivePresenter. The free edition of ActivePresenter software, intended for noncommercial use, is available for Windows and macOS. Unlike the free versions of other paid software that ordinarily limit or block important features, ActivePresenter provides full access to every feature you will need to make a high-quality screencast. After capturing your screencast using the software, the standard offering of video editing tools will allow you to cut, crop, and merge different portions of the recording. You can change the volume level and speed up or slow down the playback of your recording before exporting. You can also annotate a video file by adding shapes or image overlays and inserting closed captioning. The cursor effects options let you choose whether to display the movement of your cursor on the screen or add attention-grabbing effects such as having a ripple of circles appear each time you click something on screen. A final, edited screencast can be exported into the most commonly used video format, MP4, or you can choose from other popular formats, such as WebM, MKV, AVI, and WMV.

In the ActivePresenter editor, you can work with multiple layers, also referred to as tracks. This is the only free software that includes this feature. Support for multiple layers is helpful in situations where, after recording a

Table 4.1   Recommended Software for Screencasting

	Operating System(s)	**Price**
ActivePresenter	Windows, Mac	Free, $199
Jing	Windows, Mac	Free
Screencast-O-Matic	Windows, Mac, Chromebook	Free, $18/year
Camtasia	Windows, Mac	$169
PowerPoint	Windows, Mac	Included in Office 365
Xbox App	Windows	Free
QuickTime Player	Mac	Free
Screen Record	iOS	Free
AZ Screen Recorder	Android	Free

screencast, you realize that you left something out of your narration that you need to include. Ordinarily you would need to rerecord that portion of your screencast to include the missing narration, cut out the corresponding portion from the original video, and paste the new portion in its place. With multiple layer support, you can simply record the missing audio, stretch out a section of the video where you want to add that audio, and overlay it onto your existing screencast video track.

ActivePresenter also supports recording internal computer audio, the sounds that would ordinarily come out of your speakers. This feature comes in handy when creating tutorials or playing videos within your screencast. A paid Pro version of the software ($199 with education discount) offers the ability to create interactive quizzes and tutorials that can be exported in HTML5 format to be viewable and interacted with in any Web browser. The Pro version also supports export to PowerPoint, Word, and other document formats, along with advanced audio and video effects.

Jing. This free, easy-to-use screencasting tool from TechSmith is popular with reference librarians. Available for Windows and macOS, Jing allows you to make quick screencasts of up to five minutes that can then be uploaded to TechSmith's streaming video Web site (https://screencast.com) with the click of a button. After uploading, you are given a short URL to send to whomever you would like to share the video with, or you can add the link to a Web page or learning management system.

Videos cannot be edited in Jing. They can only be saved in the SWF format, which is no longer commonly used and which is not easy to edit in other software. Jing is most useful for making quick-and-dirty videos that can easily be shared without having to spend any time going through the steps of exporting a video and uploading it to a streaming site or learning management system.

Screencast-O-Matic. This Web-based service allows you to record screencasts of up to 15 minutes for free on Windows, macOS, or Chromebooks and includes limited features such as highlighting the cursor and showing visual effects for clicking. The free version does not include any editing tools. After downloading a small Screencast-O-Matic application, you must initiate the recording from the service's Web site. Once you finish recording, the screencast can be saved as an MP4 file, uploaded to YouTube, or uploaded to Screencast-O-Matic's sharing Web site (https://screencast-o-matic.com).

Users can subscribe to the Screencast-O-Matic Video Editor for $18 per year that comes with a Pro version of the recording application. The Video Editor includes tools to cut, crop, and merge different sections of your screencast. You can also insert other video files from your computer into your screencast. Additional features of the paid version include the ability to record internal computer audio, add annotation overlays, adjust the volume of the audio track, insert audio effects, and choose from additional cursor effects.

Camtasia. This paid screencasting and video editing application for Windows and macOS is made by TechSmith, the makers of Jing, and contains a full complement of standard video editing tools and advanced editing and design options. Camtasia allows you to work with multiple layered audio and video tracks and makes it easy to separate the video from the audio in a recording. The basic editing tools available in the free video editors previously mentioned are included, along with several cursor effects and audio effects. Camtasia also has a similar set of advanced features as ActivePresenter Pro, including the ability to design interactive quizzes, drawing and annotation, and cursor effects, along with direct uploading to YouTube and other streaming sites. The video editor includes many advanced audio and video effects. A 15-day trial is available, and education pricing is $169.

PowerPoint. As mentioned earlier, Office 365 subscribers can record narration directly into their PowerPoint presentations, and the audio and timing for each slide will be saved with that slide. A fully narrated presentation can then be exported as a video. In the video, the audio will be synced correctly, and slides will advance using the saved timing.

Built-In Screen Recorders: Xbox App, QuickTime Player, Screen Record. The Windows, macOS, and iOS operating systems contain built-in screen recording functionality. In all three operating system, you can record a screencast to save in MP4 format. However, these built-in screen recorders do not include any editing tools.

In Windows 10, you can use the built-in Xbox App to create screencasts. The app's Game DVR feature is intended to be used to record live gameplay of Xbox games, but it can be used to record the live movement and narration in any application. In macOS, you can launch QuickTime Player and select File > New Screen Recording to create a screencast. In either Windows or macOS, be sure to select your preferred microphone as your audio source if you plan to record narration. Otherwise, the computer's built-in microphone may be chosen by default, resulting in low-quality audio.

To enable screen recording with audio in iOS, you need to first add the Screen Record functionality to your Control Center. Begin by going to

Settings > Control Center, scroll down to Screen Record, and tap the green plus sign. It will now always be available in your Control Center, where you can tap on it to begin recording just the screen or press down and hold on your screen to choose the option to also record audio. The video will be saved in the Camera Roll of your Photos app. From within the Photos app, you can trim off the beginning or ending of the recording.

AZ Screen Recorder. The Android operating system does not have a built-in screen recording feature, but the free AZ Screen Recorder app works well and allows you to pause your recording. You can also annotate or draw on the screen while recording and trim off any unneeded beginning or ending portions of the video.

Recommended Microphones

If your school's audiovisual, media, or educational technology department does not lend out microphones, a good-quality microphone is worth purchasing if you have some funds available to support your instruction. USB headsets with microphones are a low-cost option for screencasting, although they will not provide as high-quality audio as any of the stationary microphones mentioned later in these recommendations. Stationary microphones are generally of a higher quality because they are designed to record speech, singing, and musical instruments.

For the purposes of creating a screencast for your students, the quality of the audio captured by any USB headset will likely be sufficient. One benefit of using a USB headset is that you can easily stand up and move around while recording if you prefer not to be seated in front of a stationary microphone. The Logitech USB Headset H390 provides good audio quality for around $20, while the Sennheiser PC 8 provides better quality for about $35.

Blue Microphones makes two popular USB stationary microphones that are used by many educators when making screencasts: the Snowball and the Yeti. The Snowball is the smaller and less expensive option ($69.99) that offers cardioid and omnidirectional recording patterns. For recording a single voice, which you will mostly likely be doing, the cardioid pattern picks up sound from the front of the microphone while canceling out sounds coming from behind the microphone. You can use omnidirectional to record all the surrounding sound, if, for instance, someone else is recording with you. The Snowball also comes in a less expensive version ($49.99), iCE, that supports only cardioid recording.

The higher-quality and more expensive Yeti ($129.99) includes four recording pattern settings: stereo, cardioid, omnidirectional, and bidirectional. The stereo pattern picks up sound from the front, left, and right of the microphone while reducing pickup from behind it. Bidirectional picks up from the front and back and is best used when recording an interview with a person sitting across from you.

Audio Lectures Accompanied by Presentation Slides

An alternative to creating screencasts or recording an in-class lecture video is to give students two separate pieces of Content that, when combined, have the same effect for conveying information: an audio recording similar to a screencast's narration and a presentation slide deck. Students can play the audio lecture file while viewing the slide deck, which will be helpful to aural, visual, and independent learners. This option can be quicker and less cumbersome for some instructors than learning to use screencasting and video editing software. Any of the previously mentioned presentation tools can be used to create the slide deck, and a number of recommended audio recording software applications are described in "Recommended Audio Recording Software."

Tips for Audio Lectures Accompanied by Presentation Slides

Review the presentation software and screencasting tips because most also apply to this technique. In addition, it is important to give students an aural cue to advance slides such as saying "next slide." It is best to distribute your presentation as a PDF to students because all computers and mobile devices have built-in PDF viewing support. Otherwise, your students will need to install an application to view the original file type, such as PowerPoint, if they do not already have software installed that supports that file type.

Recommended Audio Recording Software

Audacity. This open-source application is a popular free option for audio recording and editing in Windows and macOS. Audacity allows you to export your audio in the commonly used MP3 format that can be played on any device, along with numerous other audio formats. The application contains a broad offering of editing features, most of which are more advanced than you will need to record and edit an audio lecture. Audacity may seem complicated to use at first due to all the available features, but after a brief review of the documentation published online, you will find that basic recording and editing are not difficult.

Voice Recorder. Windows 10 comes with a built-in Voice Recorder application that allows you to record audio files in M4A format, an audio format popularized by iTunes and playable on any computer or mobile device. With Voice Recorder, you can also pause while recording and edit out any portion of the audio file with the trim feature. If you are using a USB microphone, make sure that it is selected as the audio source.

QuickTime Player. On a Mac, you can use the built-in QuickTime application to record audio in M4A format and trim the resulting audio file. After launching the application, select File > New Audio Recording. If you are using a USB microphone, make sure that it is selected as the audio source.

GarageBand. This full-feature audio recording and editing application made by Apple is available for free from the Mac App Store. It supports multiple audio tracks and contains many advanced audio editing features.

iOS Voice Memos. This app comes with all iOS mobile devices and allows you to record, trim, and save audio in M4A format. Use earbuds or headphones with an in-line microphone for better audio quality compared to speaking directly into the device's built-in microphone.

Audio Recorder. Most Android devices have a built-in voice recorder app designed by the device's manufacturer. In addition, Audio Recorder from Sony is available for free, is easy to use, and does not include advertisements or in-app purchases. Use earbuds or headphones with an in-line microphone for better audio quality compared to speaking directly into the device's built-in microphone.

Use of Third-Party Video and Audio Content

You can save yourself a lot of time and effort by using existing video and audio content created by other educators and vendors that they have made openly available online. A quick YouTube search may uncover a few videos that explain important concepts in the course in a similar manner to how you would explain them. You can assign those videos to your students if you are comfortable with using other educators' Content. At the very least, the videos can serve as inspiration for a screencast you may be thinking of creating.

Many vendors have also created tutorial videos that demonstrate how to use their electronic resources. Assigning these videos rather than creating your own tutorials can be a big time-saver if you find that the existing videos cover a similar scope to what you would explain in a tutorial. If you feel that certain points you would like to make are missing, such as caveats about using some features in an electronic resource, you can create an additional screencast that serves as an addendum to the vendor-created videos rather than duplicating much of what the vendor has already demonstrated.

Tips for Use of Third-Party Video and Audio Content

If a vendor has not created a video that discusses a resource or feature that you are considering creating a screencast about, you may first want to contact your vendor representative and ask whether the training department can make that video for you and other customers to use.

Some instructors are wary of using Content that others have created because they do not want students to get the impression that they are not willing to make that Content themselves. There is no need to worry about this because students nowadays are quite accustomed to using a variety of online streaming videos as how-to tutorials, and your assigning someone else's Content will not seem unusual to them.

Interactive Tutorials

A valuable tool for research skills development is using interactive tutorials that blend Content and Process. Interactive tutorials can include a combination of text, graphics, video, audio, and interactive exercises that allows students to learn a new concept or skill and then to apply those skills to help them make sense of it. In an interactive tutorial, you ordinarily first explain how to use a resource, then show it to the viewers through a demonstration, and lastly invite the viewers to try it out themselves. Some software is designed specifically for the creation of these types of interactive learning objects, such as ActivePresenter Pro and Camtasia. If you do not have access to such software, you can create a screencast tutorial video and then invite the viewers to complete an active learning exercise where they apply what they have just learned in the video. If you use an interactive or screencast video tutorial in a course, have students submit some type of Product to show that they successfully completed the exercise as part of the tutorial. This can be done either as a submission within a tutorial or through some other means where they submit it directly to you, such as through a quizzing tool or online form. Interactive tutorials accommodate the learning styles of visual, aural, read-write, kinesthetic, active, and independent learners.

Recommended Resources for Interactive Tutorials

In addition to ActivePresenter Pro and Camtasia, you can also use TED-Ed, a Web-based lesson creation platform from the organization behind TED Talks and Conferences, to create interactive tutorials. TED-Ed allows you to build a lesson around YouTube videos, including those you create and upload yourself, and ask multiple-choice, short-answer, or long-response questions related to the information discussed in that video. Instead of placing the quiz-type questions directly into the video, the questions appear on the screen in the area surrounding the video. This is an easy way to make the learning process interactive without having to design a more complicated tutorial with a software application.

LIST OF RECOMMENDED RESOURCES

For ease of reference, the following list contains all of the various content-creation resources recommended in this chapter, organized by the type of content.

- *Presentation Slides:*
  - Microsoft PowerPoint
  - Google Slides
  - Prezi
  - Apple Keynote
- *Still Images:*
  - Creative Commons Search (https://search.creativecommons.org)
  - Google Images (https://images.google.com)
  - Bing Image Search (http://www.bing.com/images/)

- Wikimedia Commons (https://commons.wikimedia.org)
- Everystockphoto.com
- Pixabay (https://www.pixabay.com)
- Pexels (https://www.pexels.com)
- Unsplash (https://unsplash.com)
- FreePhotos.cc (https://freephotos.cc/)
- StockJo (https://www.stockjo.com)
- Shutterstock (https://www.shutterstock.com)
- iStock by Getty Images (https://www.istockphoto.com)
- 123RF (https://www.123rf.com)
- Adobe Stock (https://stock.adobe.com)
- *Comics and Cartoons:*
  - GoComics (http://www.gocomics.com)
  - azcentral (http://comics.azcentral.com)
- *Memes:*
  - Meme Generator (https://memegenerator.net)
  - Imgflip (https://imgflip.com)
  - Make a Meme (https://makeameme.org)
- *Tables and Charts:*
  - Microsoft Word
  - Microsoft Excel
  - Google Docs
  - Google Sheets
  - Apple Pages
  - Apple Numbers
- *Diagrams:*
  - Microsoft Word
  - Google Docs
  - Apple Pages
  - Venngage (https://venngage.com)
  - Canva (https://www.canva.com)
  - Infogram (https://infogram.com)

- Visme (https://www.visme.co)
- Piktochart (https://piktochart.com)
- *Pictographs:*
  - Flaticon (https://www.flaticon.com)
  - The Noun Project (https://thenounproject.com)
  - Iconfinder (https://www.iconfinder.com/free_icons)
  - Windows 10 emoji picker
  - macOS emoji picker
  - Chromebook emoji picker
- *Infographics:*
  - Microsoft Word
  - Google Docs
  - Apple Pages
  - Venngage (https://venngage.com)
  - Canva (https://www.canva.com)
  - Infogram (https://infogram.com)
  - Visme (https://www.visme.co)
  - Piktochart (https://piktochart.com)
- *Graphic Organizers:*
  - Venngage (https://venngage.com)
  - Canva (https://www.canva.com)
  - Infogram (https://infogram.com)
  - Visme (https://www.visme.co)
  - Piktochart (https://piktochart.com)
  - Coggle (https://coggle.it)
  - MindMup (https://www.mindmup.com)
  - Bubbl.us (https://bubbl.us)
  - Freemind (http://freemind.sourceforge.net)
  - Freeplane (https://www.freeplane.org)
  - XMind (https://www.xmind.net)
  - Mindomo (https://www.mindomo.com)

- *Screencasting (Software):*
  - ActivePresenter
  - Jing
  - Screencast-O-Matic
  - Camtasia
  - PowerPoint
  - Xbox App (Windows 10)
  - QuickTime Player (macOS)
  - Screen Record (iOS)
  - AZ Screen Recorder (Android)
- *Screencasting (Microphones):*
  - Logitech USB Headset H390
  - Sennheiser PC 8 USB Headset
  - Blue Snowball
  - Blue Yeti
- *Audio Lectures:*
  - Audacity
  - Voice Recorder (Windows 10)
  - QuickTime Player (macOS)
  - GarageBand (macOS)
  - iOS Voice Memos
  - Audio Recorder (Android)
- *Interactive Tutorials:*
  - ActivePresenter Pro
  - Camtasia
  - TED-Ed (https://ed.ted.com)

FIVE

Techniques and Tools for Differentiating Process

Creating Process learning objects or activities is the stage of differentiation that will likely be least familiar to you because traditional instruction primarily focuses on Content and Product, leaving students on their own to make sense of the information they are learning. Students benefit greatly from the clear path toward mastery you provide when offering active learning exercises and experiences during this critical stage in their learning process. Students also benefit from having you available to clarify concepts and to answer questions as they arise during in-class active learning.

All of the learning objects you intend to use during the Process stage should focus on at least one learning outcome and be designed to assist students with synthesizing what they are learning while helping them acquire new knowledge and skills. Creating these learning objects may require you to plan and design activities and exercises that are not derived from any of the teaching materials that you may already be using. In this chapter, you will find several ideas for whole-class, small-group, and individual Process activities. You should ideally give students the choice of at least two Process learning objects each time you use active learning, and each learning object should accommodate a different set of learning styles from among those in Figure 4.1 (page 47). However, you may find that at certain times you would like all of the students to be doing the same Process activity. If this occurs frequently in your course, make sure to vary the type of activity so that different learning styles are being accommodated each time. It can also be helpful to students to let them know which learning outcomes are the focus of each activity, especially with small-group and individual activities.

Process may also be the stage that will take the most getting used to if you decide to transition from spending a large portion of your classroom time passively lecturing to dedicating the majority of that time to active learning experiences and exercises, such as in a flipped classroom. Academic instruction librarians will have an easier time with making this transition than other instructors in higher education because they are already accustomed to working alongside student patrons to assist them in the library. Nonetheless, the transition from a quiet classroom where students are passively listening as you lecture to an active classroom where students are working on exercises either alone or with peers does take some time to adapt to. Learning how to effectively manage a classroom in which everyone is working on an activity and many students may be trying to get your attention requires you to develop some new skills that will be discussed in the "Classroom Management" section in this chapter.

WHOLE-GROUP ACTIVITIES

It is easy to get the impression that whole-group instruction does not fit within the goals of differentiation because of the emphasis placed on breaking with traditional teaching techniques, such as lectures, where students are doing the same thing in the classroom at the same time. However, a variety of differentiation techniques that involve the whole class working together rather than individually or in small groups can more actively engage several learning styles that are underserved by traditional instruction. Be mindful of the fact that opting for one of the techniques described here will mean that students will not have a choice of doing other activities during that time because everyone is engaging in the same activity, so these should be used sparingly or for short periods of time instead of for the full class session.

Review and Discussion

Beginning each class session with a brief review of the Content that students should have covered before class that day, followed by a guided discussion about the key points contained in that Content, is a good approach to help students start to make sense of what they are learning. The review should not be an attempt to quickly reteach the material from the Content but instead should presume that all of the students are already familiar with the information and allow you to emphasize the most important points from the Content. The Review and Discussion phase does not need to occupy much class time and can be used as the first activity of a class session to get students started on their synthesis of the material before moving on to other Process activities. The review portion of this activity accommodates the learning preference of visual, aural, and dependent learners, while the discussion is most appealing to aural, participative, and collaborative learners.

Review and Discussion can take several forms. You can deliver a mini-lecture presentation with slides that recap all of the major points from the Content. One modification of this approach that reduces any temptation to reteach the material is to have each slide contain only a title that describes one major point, below which a thought question appears that is designed to engage students in a brief discussion about that point. These questions can ask students to apply what they have learned to a real-world scenario, invite them to opine on the topic, or ask them for examples of how they have encountered that topic in their lives.

Your review can also take as simple a format as putting an outline of all of the topics covered in the Content for that class on the board or displaying them on a projection screen, followed by a discussion centered on a series of questions, as just mentioned. With this approach, you are not identifying what topic a question pertains to but allowing students to reference an outline that shows all of the possible topics.

Review and Discussion also allows you to quickly assess whether a large portion of the students are not understanding a particular point that you may then want to reteach on the spot. Reteaching Content should be avoided if possible, but you may want to go to class every day prepared to briefly reteach any of the concepts, if needed. If you created a slide deck or other visual material for the Content for this lesson, you may want to bring those files with you to class on a flash drive in case you need to reteach a particular point.

Debates

Holding a debate in the classroom related to a concept presented in the Content is a useful way to examine the concept and engage students in critically analyzing surrounding issues. Even in situations where the Content has stressed the importance of only one side of an issue, such as how plagiarism is unacceptable in an academic setting, inviting students to debate the concept can emphasize the importance of the prevailing view while helping students understand that opposing views can exist. Students with many different learning styles are accommodated by this technique, including aural, kinesthetic, participative, collaborative, competitive, and dependent learners.

You can inform students well in advance of class that they will be taking part in a debate that day and assign each student to a group, either for or against a position related to that day's topics. Or you can wait until class to let students know. If you inform students in advance, you may want to ask them all to arrive to class with a list of points they think would be valuable to raise in the debate. You may also suggest that they get together with other classmates in their group to begin discussing their arguments and rebuttals to anticipated arguments from the opposing side. However, students will benefit from having you available in person to guide them through their debate preparations and to make sure they are on the right track with their processing of what they are learning, and this benefit will be lost if they prepare outside class. Preparing outside class can also be quite time-consuming for students.

Because the focus of this section is on whole-class activities that can be entirely done in the classroom, the following suggestions will assume that students have not prepared for the debate outside class. After presenting the statement that will be debated and explaining the format, divide the class into two teams and assign each team the role of arguing for or against the statement. Given that the debate exercise is meant to assist students in making sense of what they are learning, the time the teams spend preparing for their arguments and rebuttals may be more valuable to their learning process than the time they will spend debating. Allocate at least 15 minutes for the teams to prepare their arguments, and let them know that you are available to answer questions they may have during their preparation.

Have one or two students from each team present at least three arguments in support of their position in no more than five minutes. Begin with the team arguing in favor of the statement, followed by the team arguing against it. Once both teams have presented their arguments, give the students 10 minutes to prepare their response or rebuttal. Then each team will present their rebuttal for three minutes, beginning with the team arguing in favor.

After the second rebuttal is presented, it is important to have a debriefing and discussion following the debate. You can ask students about which arguments from each side were most convincing, inquire whether there were any additional arguments that either team identified but decided not to include among the three, and ask students about their experience in participating in the exercise, including what aspects were most challenging or unexpected in preparing for the debate and rebuttal. You do not have to poll the class at the end of the debriefing to decide which team won, although it may be unsatisfying for competitive learning style students if no winner is declared. During the debrief, it is important to stress to students that, although the groups in the debate are asked to take polar opposite views, some individuals may hold views that fall between the two being debated.

If students are not told in advance about the debate, then one team may have an advantage if the Content is strongly in support of one side. Remind the students of this imbalance and that one team did not have the opportunity to thoroughly research arguments in preparation for the debate. You may even want to include some discussion about this imbalance during the debriefing.

Demonstrations

Leading the class in a demonstration of how to use a print or electronic resource or of how to begin applying another information literacy skill that they are developing is an effective way to guide students in the process of beginning to make sense of what they are learning. During the demonstration, you should ask students questions related to the skill being demonstrated to assess how far along they are in their processing of the information in the unit. Demonstrations appeal to visual, aural, participative, collaborative, and dependent learners. If you are demonstrating an electronic resource and invite students to follow along on their personal laptops or mobile devices, this will also appeal to kinesthetic learners.

Demonstrations can also be a useful tool to review a skill near the end of a unit. In this case, you can introduce a question or task and ask the class to guide you in how to answer it. This exercise offers students an opportunity to review the reasoning process and skills related to the question or task while collaborating and showing you their mastery of the material. You can also ask for a student to volunteer to take your place in the demonstration while the other students guide the volunteer through the steps to answer the question.

Group Presentations

In lieu of your preparing a review and leading a discussion at the beginning of each unit, you can assign a small group of a few students to create a review presentation to deliver in class that will last five to 10 minutes. The presenters should write questions to ask the class during their review and discussion and should be prepared to answer questions from the class, with your assistance when needed. This technique functions as both a whole-class and a small-group activity and accommodates the learning preferences of visual, aural, read-write, kinesthetic, participative, collaborative, and dependent students.

At the beginning of the semester, you can divide students into groups and assign each group one unit where they will be expected to deliver a review presentation, or you can select the students a week in advance of the class where they will present. Most students will already be familiar with how to use at least one of the presentation tools mentioned in Chapter Four. Nonetheless, you may want to share the list of recommended presentation resources from Chapter Four with them in the event they are not familiar with any presentation software or would like to learn to use a new tool.

SMALL-GROUP ACTIVITIES

When many educators think of active learning exercises and experiences, they imagine a scenario where students collaborate in small groups in the classroom under the guidance and supervision of the instructor. These small-group experiences give students the opportunity to work together to make sense of what they are learning, share their understanding with their peers, and learn from one another. These activities allow students to experience the comradery of mastering new material together, while giving them an opportunity to gauge their progress against their peers' understanding. As students work on small-group activities, you can spend time checking in on each group and answering questions in a setting where students will feel more comfortable asking questions compared to a traditional instruction environment because they are not interrupting you while you are in front of the classroom.

Think-Pair-Share

This simple small-group activity involves students working in pairs as they begin to Process the information they are learning. The activity starts with the instructor posing a question to the class, followed by two to five minutes where students think about the question on their own while jotting down a few points on a piece of paper. Each student should then be paired with another student, and, together, they compare and discuss their responses or thoughts related to the question for five to 10 minutes, depending on the complexity of the question.

You should then call on random students to share with the whole class some of the main points that were part of their comparison and discussion. This allows all students to benefit from their peers' discussions since some pairings may identify additional important points that other pairings do not. After calling on a few students, you can fill in any points that the students may have missed. Think-Pair-Share is an effective Process learning object because students begin by making sense of the information on their own, followed by further refinement of their processing with a partner, and hopefully additional clarification during the whole-class sharing portion. This activity appeals to aural, kinesthetic, participative, collaborative, and dependent students.

Group Presentations

As described in the Whole-Group Activities section, you may want to have small groups of a few students each deliver brief review presentations to the class. See that section for more information. Group presentations can also be used as a summative or formative assessment during the Product stage of differentiation.

Comparing Resources and Results

One of the most popular small-group activities in differentiated instruction is to have groups of three to five students work on answering a problem or completing a task collaboratively. This approach is especially useful at times when students are learning about multiple research resources. Begin by posing a question to the class that will require them to use print or electronic resources, by displaying it on either the board or a projection screen, or distributing a handout with the question or a series of questions. After dividing the class into small groups, students can spend a few minutes strategizing together about how to approach answering the question before they individually conduct the necessary research. While the students are working in their groups, you should walk around the room, check in on how each group is doing, and ask whether they have any questions. You may even find that students call out to get your attention when they have questions. Once students have found an answer or the allotted amount of time has passed, the students should discuss their research process, their impressions of the resource or resources they used, and their final answers.

You can try a few variations to this technique in different situations. If students are learning to use multiple resources at the same time, you can instruct the groups to have each student use a different resource so that, once they are done, they can compare the features of each resource and discuss its ease of use. If there are multiple questions, you can instruct students to rotate what resource they are using for each question so that they can experience using a few different resources during the exercise. You can also assign one resource to each group and then, after each group has completed the task and had a discussion among themselves, you can ask one representative from each group to share the group's impressions of that resource with the whole class. This allows each group to have a shared experience with a single resource while learning about the other resources from their peers in other groups. If there are multiple questions and time permits, you can then assign a different resource to each group for each subsequent question.

You may want to group students based on their learning styles and preferences that were revealed by the preassessment. Placing students with similar learning styles together can be beneficial if you expect that the group will work more smoothly because they have similar ways of learning. You can also group students with complementary learning styles together, such as collaborative and dependent students. One additional approach is to place independent learners with collaborative learners so that the independent students can work on their collaboration skills.

Because this technique involves some collaboration and discussion among group members and some time spent working alone with a resource, it accommodates the learning needs of visual, aural, read-write, kinesthetic, participative, collaborative, dependent, and independent learners. Some students with competitive learning traits may also find it appealing to have each student work with a different resource to determine which is the most useful or work quickly to be the first one to find a correct answer.

Preparing Study Materials

Another activity that can be valuable to students of varied learning styles is to have them work together in small groups to prepare study materials. Many students have the impression that the only way to study for a final Product, like a test or exam, is to reread their notes and memorize important points. Adopting this Process technique can help students learn about how their peers prepare to study and expose them to different study tools.

You can assign students with similar or complementary learning styles, as identified in the preassessment, to the same group so that they can learn study approaches that work for those who share their learning style. On the other hand, if you assign students with different learning styles to each group, some may learn new Process techniques that they had not previously considered and that may end up working well for them. The conversations among group members may help some students further make sense of what they are learning as they work together to prepare a variety of study materials.

Before students begin working together on preparing study materials, you can spend 10 to 15 minutes describing several study techniques they may want to consider adopting. You can explain to students how they can use flash cards, graphic organizers, condensed outlines, study groups, and other approaches while they study. Some students may already be using some of these techniques without realizing that not everyone is aware of them. This Process technique works well for visual, read-write, kinesthetic, participative, collaborative, and dependent learning styles but may not work as well for others. If you use this activity more than once in the classroom, you can give students the option to work alone after the first time to accommodate independent learners.

INDIVIDUAL ACTIVITIES

Accommodating independent learners with differentiated instruction can be challenging. It may not be feasible to give them the option to choose a different learning activity when you are doing a whole-group activity. You may want to give students the choice to opt out of small-group activities and instead complete a modified version of the exercise on their own in order to allow independent learners to decide for themselves whether they would like to collaborate with their peers. Some of the Process activities such as Comparing Resources and Responses and Preparing Study Materials involve students spending some of the allotted time working on their own, accommodating independent learners for a portion of the activity. Also keep in mind that the time students spend engaging with the Content learning objects and many of the formative assessment Products mentioned in Chapter Six are individual activities that appeal to independent learners; so, although you may not be able to fully accommodate them during some Process activities, they are accommodated in other areas of differentiated instruction.

CLASSROOM MANAGEMENT

Adopting differentiated instruction involves major shifts not only in how classroom time is spent but also in the structure and function of the learning environment, and these shifts may take some time to adjust to. It is important to prepare yourself and your students for these changes. Either on the first day of class or on the first day that you will be differentiating a lesson, you should take time to explain differentiated instruction to your class and emphasize that it is a student-centered approach where all students are expected to be active and responsible participants in their own learning. Explain that the time you spend together will no longer be focused on your conveying information to them. Instead, the time will be spent on their making sense of what they are learning and working collaboratively to master the learning outcomes. Administering a preassessment will serve as the first sign that you are committed to a student-centered teaching approach.

Impress upon students that in your preparations for class you are investing time into creating different ways for them to engage with Content, new Process activities, and a variety of ways for them to assess their own learning so that they can have a greater opportunity to succeed in the course. Emphasize that it is especially important for them to complete Content learning objects before class because you will no longer be lecturing and they will be expected to have already engaged with the new material before class. Remind them that, as adult learners, they are expected to behave responsibly and remain focused on what they are learning.

Because students will no longer be spending the majority of their time facing forward as you lecture while they take notes, each differentiated class session may need to begin with students rearranging their desks in order to accommodate the active learning that will be happening that day. If you are requiring all students to do the same small-group activity, you may want to determine which students will be in which group in advance and write the names of the members of each group on the board or project the list onto a screen in the front of the classroom. This way, when students arrive they can begin to arrange themselves into their groups before class begins. If a small-group activity is one of two or more Process options, students will first need to select their learning objects before rearranging their desks.

A noisy classroom is unavoidable when students are working in small groups. If you are concerned that the noise will bother nearby classrooms, remind students to keep their voices low out of consideration for students in those classrooms. While students are working on small-group activities, you should be walking around the room not only to make yourself available for students to ask questions but also to check in on each group to make sure that they are working on the exercise and not chatting about unrelated topics or distracted by other things they may be doing on their laptops. Although off-topic conversations and other distractions will occur, students ordinarily remain engaged with the activity they are collaborating on with their peers. If you find that too many students are not concentrating on an exercise, you can pause their group work and have a class-wide discussion about each group's progress. This will help refocus the students and show any groups that are not fully focusing on the exercise that they have fallen behind compared to the others.

It will not take long for you and the students to acclimate to the changes that come along with differentiated instruction. As students witness how the approach benefits their learning, they will become increasingly invested in what you are all working on.

SIX

Techniques and Tools for Differentiating Product

The Product phase of differentiating instruction involves evaluating students' progress toward achieving a unit's or course's learning outcomes. If you have taught before, you are already accustomed to designing unit- or course-end tests, exams, or projects as the graded summative assessment. Product checks your students' final progress toward mastering the new knowledge and skills they are expected to learn. In this case, designing such Product learning objects may be the easiest phase of adopting differentiated instruction because up front you only need to revise the learning object to offer students options for how they prepare and submit the Product. The more challenging aspect is ensuring that grading is consistent regardless of variations in the format of the final Product. Using a comprehensive grading rubric that is not dependent on format is the key to fair grading and will be discussed in the "Summative Assessments" section in this chapter.

Administering formative assessment tools, such as practice quizzes, while students are still in the process of learning new material is an effective way for you and your students both to measure their progress toward achieving all the learning outcomes and to identify areas that need more attention. Providing students with feedback on their progress is a necessary part of the formative assessment process. This feedback can either be automated by several of the recommended resources or may require you to take the time to review student submissions. Many instructors opt not to use formative assessment learning objects because they have limited time to dedicate to reviewing them and providing feedback. If you decide to include formative assessments in the Product phase of your differentiated instruction, the next section will provide a more in-depth explanation of their use, along with tips and recommended resources for their implementation. If you prefer to not use formative assessments, you can skip the next section and go on to the "Summative Assessments" section.

FORMATIVE ASSESSMENTS

One aspect of Product that may be new to you is the inclusion of formative assessments. These are usually low-stakes or no-stakes (ungraded) learning objects, such as practice quizzes or practice tests, that you and your students can use to check their progress toward mastering the knowledge and skills they are expected to learn and to determine their strengths and weaknesses. Assessing students' progress can help you modify your teaching plan by identifying subtopics that many students are still not clear on, signaling where you may want to introduce additional Process learning objects designed to improve their knowledge acquisition or skills development in those areas.

Because the purpose of formative assessments is to determine how far a student has progressed toward achieving the desired learning outcomes, grades should not be given based on how well a student performs. If you are concerned that students may not take the time to complete formative assessments or may not put in their full effort, you may want to motivate students by allocating some points for completion of the assessment or for the thoroughness of the answers given. An alternative is to make formative assessments optional and not allocate any points to their completion, allowing each student to decide whether to complete the assessment.

A feedback mechanism is essential for effectively using formative assessments. Feedback should be tied to the learning outcomes because they are the achievement standards by which students will eventually be measured on the final, summative Product(s). Some types of formative assessment learning objects can be designed to allow students to correct the assessment themselves, once completed. This way, students will have immediate feedback indicating the areas where they are close to mastery and those where they still need to apply more significant effort. For example, you can provide an answer key along with a practice quiz so that students can self-correct the quiz. The answer key should identify which learning outcome is being assessed by each question.

Many of the technology-based tools recommended for formative assessments can immediately correct the assessment and provide students their scores, along with explanations of the correct answers. If you prefer to correct a formative assessment, be sure to return it to students quickly so that they can adjust where they are focusing their efforts during their learning process. If the class meets once a week or less frequently, then it is recommended that you e-mail students feedback before the next class.

The majority of formative assessments are written exercises that are the most appealing to the needs of read-write, participative, and dependent learners. Some formative assessments can be modified to better accommodate students with other learning styles, and those instances will be noted shortly.

Practice Quizzes

A short practice quiz at the end of a unit is a useful formative assessment that may not be too time-consuming for you to prepare. A quiz with multiple-choice and fill-in-the-blank questions can easily be self-corrected by students using an answer key that should state which learning outcome is assessed by each question. All of the recommended online tools in this section are capable of automatically correcting quizzes. If the relationship between the question and the learning outcome is not entirely obvious, you should explain it on the answer key or in the explanatory text in an online quizzing tool. You can also include short-answer questions on a practice quiz that you can either correct or have students self-correct using an answer key that includes a sample answer.

Tips for Practice Quizzes

Along with each answer, consider including citations or references to where in the Content learning objects students can find the material relevant to that question so that they can review it if they get the question wrong.

Recommended Resources for Practice Quizzes

Learning Management System Quizzing Tool. Your institution's learning management system may include a quizzing tool that allows you to build formative assessments with true-or-false, multiple-choice, and fill-in-the-blank questions that are automatically corrected upon submission. These tools ordinarily allow instructors to include explanatory text to accompany each right answer. Within the explanatory text, you can also include references to the learning outcomes and related Content learning objects.

Google Forms. Google's G Suite of free browser-based apps includes Google Forms, which is most commonly used for collecting information and administering surveys. The platform also includes a quiz creation tool that can be accessed by opening a new form, clicking the Settings gear icon in the upper right corner, and selecting Quizzes > Make this a quiz. Question types include multiple-choice, short-answer, grid, and long-response questions. An answer key can be created for automatic correction of all question types except for long-response questions. You can choose to have students' corrected quizzes displayed upon submission, along with the explanatory text. There is no limit to how many students can take a quiz. You can also generate a report of all submissions to help you identify areas where a large number of students are behind in their progress toward achieving the learning outcomes.

Socrative. This online quizzing platform is popular with educators at all grade levels and free for up to 50 students. Socrative is an easy-to-use tool for designing quizzes that can be automatically corrected by the system. Students receive immediate feedback, with their scores and explanatory text displayed right after they finish. For each quiz, you can generate reports for individual students or the entire class.

Survey Monkey. This leading online survey platform contains a built-in quiz creation tool that makes it easy to set up quizzes with up to 10 multiple-choice, short-answer, grid, and long-response questions. When creating a new survey, select Quiz from the list of categories to launch the quizzing tool. A report summarizing the responses submitted can also be generated. As many as 100 students can take a quiz that can be graded automatically, but customized feedback with explanatory text is available only with a paid subscription. Survey Monkey's three pricing tiers for educational subscriptions begin at $22 per month (at the time of writing this book), and all three plans support feedback with explanatory text.

Practice Tests

If you have taught the same course for several years, you may already have a previously administered unit test or final exam that you are willing to share with students as a practice test to help assess their progress. If you do not have the time to correct a practice test, self-correcting one may be more challenging for students than a practice quiz if some questions, such as essays, involve more detailed answers compared to the limited choices students ordinarily have on a quiz. Nonetheless, it can still be helpful to give students a practice test with an answer key containing sample essays that reflect what should be included in responses that would receive full credit. If you believe a full practice test or exam would take students too much time to complete, consider sharing a portion as a formative assessment. The online quizzing tools recommended for practice quizzes can also be used for practice tests.

Minute Papers and Countdowns

You can use minute papers as a quick formative assessment tool at the end of each class to help you and the students identify the areas where they are having the most trouble. The most commonly used format for a Minute Paper is to set aside the last one to three minutes of class for students to write a brief response to each of two question prompts: "What is the most important thing you learned about the topic(s) covered in today's class?" and "What is the muddiest point left unanswered?" You can modify the first question to ask students to list more than one important thing they learned about that class's topics or instead ask students to identify a real-world application for what was learned. You can offer aural learners the option to record a brief voice memo after class to submit via e-mail in lieu of a written Minute Paper. This exercise provides students an opportunity to quickly reflect on what they have learned and what remains unclear to them.

You can collect handwritten Minute Papers as students are leaving the classroom or ask them to e-mail you their responses. Reviewing students' responses will help you determine which areas are posing the greatest challenge to them. While you should try to provide some feedback to each student, if doing so is too time-consuming, consider e-mailing the entire class general feedback that may answer some of the muddiest points or begin the next class with a discussion addressing these points.

Countdowns are a variation on the Minute Paper that may provide both you and your students a fuller picture of how they are progressing toward mastering the learning outcomes. For a Countdown, ask students to list three things they learned that they did not know before, two things that surprised them about the day's topic(s), and one example of how they plan to apply what they learned. Although you will need to allocate an additional minute or two for this formative assessment, students will benefit from spending the extra time reflecting on their learning.

3× Summarization

With 3× Summarization, you ask students to write three different summaries of what they have learned in that unit. The first summary should be 10–15 words in length, the second 30–50 words, and the third 75–100 words. You can also suggest that students begin with the longer summary and distill their points down with each revision. In order to get an accurate snapshot of their understanding, you should ask students to write these summaries without looking at their notes or any Content material. Rewriting the summaries compels students to critically analyze what they are learning and identify what they consider to be the most important takeaways from each unit. It may be too time-consuming to do this activity at the end of class, so you may want to ask students to e-mail you their three summaries after class or submit them through a learning management system.

Classroom Polling/Student Response Systems

Using a student response system in the classroom is an easy and effective way to poll your students and help them assess their progress toward the necessary knowledge acquisition and skills development. Most educators associate classroom polling with the use of clickers, small handheld devices that allow students to respond to a multiple-choice question by pressing a button to select one of the choices. Instructors open up a poll after displaying the answer choices, see the number of responses in real time, and close the poll to share the results instantaneously in front of the class. If a large number of students choose the same incorrect answer, the instructor can immediately discuss with the class why that is not the correct choice or why another choice is better. These devices and other student response systems described in this chapter are technology-assisted ways to replace students raising their hands when you are polling a classroom for their thoughts on which of a series of choices they most agree with.

One unique benefit of student response systems compared to other formative assessments is that they allow students to compare their learning progress to the rest of the class because they get to see how their peers answered the same questions. Because responses are ordinarily anonymous, students do not have to worry about being embarrassed in front of their classmates if they select the wrong answer. Those students who select an incorrect answer may also feel comforted by the fact that other students also chose that answer. If you would like to know each individual student's choices, you can ask for the device serial numbers and input them along with each student's name in the system's software to keep track of responses. This information is not displayed to the full class.

Using clickers requires your institution or each student to purchase a device in addition to purchasing a receiver to plug into a computer's USB port in order to register the students' answers. You should check with your institution's information technology or educational technology department to see whether they have already purchased a student response system or have contracted with a vendor for a subscription-based system. Your learning management system may also offer a classroom polling feature. Several free online tools for classroom polling (mentioned in the "Recommended Resources for Classroom Pooling") allow instructors to set up multiple-choice questions in advance of class. Then, during class, students can use a computer browser, smartphone, or other mobile device to choose their responses.

Recommended Resources for Classroom Polling

Several companies make clicker-based student response systems and accompanying software. The two recommended options are clicker systems from Turning Technologies and iClicker.

Turning Technologies. At the heart of Turning Technologies' offerings is the cloud-based TurningPoint platform and ResponseWare computer software, an easy-to-use combination that works with its clicker devices or students' mobile devices to collect responses. Clicker device responses are registered through the use of a wireless receiver, while students using mobile devices need to visit TurningPoint's response system in a browser and enter a session ID to participate in the polling. An add-in for PowerPoint enables instructors to build polls directly into a slide deck to avoid going back and forth between a presentation and ResponseWare software in order to start and stop polls and view the results. TurningPoint can also be integrated into several popular learning management systems, such as BlackBoard and Canvas, so that assessment responses can be directly shared with your learning management system gradebook or other assessment tracking feature. Institutions pay for TurningPoint, and they can either purchase clickers to lend to students or require that students purchase their own.

The most commonly used device from Turning Technologies is their ResponseCard, a handheld device that is approximately the size of three credit cards stacked together, with 10 buttons that accommodate up to 10 choices for each question. Turning Technologies also makes a version of the device for visually impaired students with braille on each button and vibrations to notify students when a poll opens, when their choice is registered, and when a poll closes. The QT2 response device is about the size of a smartphone and contains a full keyboard of buttons so that students can write short answer or essay responses with the device. In addition to classroom polling, the QT2 can be used for self-paced quizzes where questions appear on the device screen and students can submit multiple-choice or typed answers and continue on with a quiz without waiting for their classmates to finish answering the question.

iClicker. This student response system offers instructors the choice of a cloud-based or installed software system to create and manage classroom polls. Handheld clickers, similar to small television remote controls, can be purchased by institutions or students, or students can purchase a subscription for mobile app or browser-based access to submit their responses. Much of iClicker's features and functionality is similar to Turning Technologies' platforms, with handheld responses collected wirelessly through a receiver and learning management system integration with gradebook support. Although a PowerPoint add-in is not available, a toolbar for the iClicker computer application floats on top of whichever software application is open, so you can launch a poll without having to go to the iClicker application and then return to PowerPoint.

Two handheld device options are available from iClicker: iClicker+ and iClicker 2 remotes, each with five buttons for questions with up to five choices. No accessible remote option for visually impaired students is available. The iClicker 2 remote supports self-paced multiple-choice quizzes but does not offer text entry for short answers or essays.

Poll Everywhere. As an alternative to these two leading clicker systems, dozens of free online polling tools are available. These tools are designed for instructor and student access on either a computer or a mobile web browser, with Poll Everywhere being the most widely adopted option. The education version of Poll Everywhere is free for up to 40 responses, supports multiple-choice or short-answer responses, and includes PowerPoint integration. If you have more than 40 students, the cost for use in a course for a semester is $349, or you can opt to have each student pay $14 for a one-year subscription instead of the course fee. You can also use the paid option to administer formative or summative quizzes that the Poll Everywhere system can automatically grade for instantaneous feedback. Institutional subscriptions are also available for Poll Everywhere with the added feature of learning management system integration.

Discussion Forum Posts

Every learning management system has a built-in discussion forum feature that can be used as a formative assessment tool. Discussion forums allow you to post a topic for discussion or ask a question or a series of questions that should be addressed in each student's response. Ordinarily, every student can see all of the responses that classmates have already posted, along with any comments or feedback you share. You can also choose to provide private feedback to each student's response.

Asking your students to share their responses to short-answer questions in a discussion forum may help you better assess their progress toward mastery of the learning outcomes than is possible with a multiple-choice quiz or a brief written formative assessment. If you assign the completion of formative discussion forum posts as homework, students will likely spend more time planning their responses and analyzing the material they are learning than they would spend in completing other formative assessments, providing you with a fuller picture of their understanding of the topic or subtopics. However, you should be mindful that this type of formative assessment will be more time-consuming for students to complete than the other techniques mentioned in this section.

One common concern instructors share about using discussion forums is that a student who waits until the last minute to submit a response may look at other students' responses and paraphrase their answers, defeating the purpose of using this tool as a formative assessment. Because this certainly can occur, it is important to impress upon your students that they should write their responses without looking at anyone else's in order to be able to truly assess their progress in learning the material. Nevertheless, do encourage students to review their peers' discussion posts after they have submitted their own in order to identify any arguments they may have missed in their response. Because feedback is a necessary aspect of using formative assessments, you should also take the time to write a short response to each student, identifying subtopics they may want to review.

Student-Composed Questions

Instead of asking students to answer questions you have written, with the student-composed questions technique, you ask them to write test-like assessment questions, accompanied by an answer key or model answers. This requires students to think about what kinds of questions would elicit responses that show mastery of the material. It can be useful to ask students to create a variety of different questions, such as one short-answer, one fill-in-the-blank, and one multiple-choice question in order to help assess their understanding of the material at different levels of complexity.

Students can submit their questions via e-mail or a learning management system. Consider offering students the option to submit questions as voice recordings to accommodate aural learners. In lieu of a traditional question, visual learners may prefer the option of submitting a graphic organizer with some empty circles or boxes that the respondents have to fill in. When you review the students' submissions, you can select the best ones and compile a practice test for students to take as an additional formative assessment.

SUMMATIVE ASSESSMENTS

Summative assessments, such as a graded test or project, are meant to evaluate students' final mastery of a unit's or course's learning outcomes. They are usually given at the end of a unit or course, after students have had time to engage with the Content, process it, and work on acquiring the intended knowledge or skills. Summative assessments are ordinarily assigned a high point value because they evaluate the end result of a student's learning process.

If you have taught before and tend to use the same type of summative assessment Product from course to course, in order to differentiate that Product you only need to modify the instructions to offer students options for how they prepare and submit it. For example, if you ordinarily give a take-home, written, final exam at the end of a course, you can give students the option of submitting voice recordings in place of written responses to short-answer and essay questions or detailed flowcharts for questions about their research or reasoning processes. Although modifying instructions is easy to do, you may end up with several submissions in a format that is new to you and that will likely include the use of multimedia.

When deciding which differentiated format options to offer, take into account your comfort level with the idea of reviewing submissions containing the corresponding type(s) of multimedia and whether you believe that students will be able to fully convey their level of mastery using a particular format. If you are considering allowing collaboration on all or part of a summative assessment to accommodate collaborative learners, you should offer this option only if you believe it will not interfere with assessing students against the learning outcomes, and you should require students to disclose in their submission whether they collaborated with a classmate. The instructions for the summative assessment should specify the differentiated options available, and you may want to require students who opt for a non-text submission to inform you of that decision before they begin preparing their Product.

It may be challenging to put a system in place that will ensure fair grading regardless of the format of the summative assessment Product. Developing grading rubrics for all summative assessment Products to evaluate how well students demonstrated their mastery of the learning outcomes, regardless of the Product's format, enables you to grade all students' work fairly. The remainder of this chapter will explain how to design and use rubrics before exploring how to differentiate several types of summative assessment techniques.

Rubrics

A rubric is a set of criteria used for assessment or grading that contains descriptions of how well students demonstrated their mastery of the learning outcomes in a Product (Brookhart, 2013). Rubrics can be used to evaluate a student's performance on the Product as a whole (holistic rubrics) or to measure their achievement of each learning outcome being assessed (analytic rubrics). Rubrics use scales, ordinarily of three to six gradations, where each gradation is accompanied by a description of how fully a student's work must demonstrate mastery in order to merit being placed at that point on the scale. For example, on a three-point scale used to assess how well a student demonstrated mastery of one learning outcome, the highest point would be accompanied by a description of full mastery, the middle point would reflect partial mastery, and the lowest point would indicate little to no mastery. Rubrics should not be used for questions where there are clear right answers, such as multiple-choice or fill-in-the-blank questions.

Strictly adhering to a rubric when evaluating summative assessments reduces the subjectivity of grading because all students are being measured against a predetermined set of criteria. Using rubrics helps eliminate the risk of grading students differently based on the amount of effort you perceive a student put into preparing their Product or on whether you find the student's writing style or choice of multimedia elements appealing. Instead, the only thing that matters is whether students demonstrate that they have mastered the learning outcomes. Rubrics also help you save time when providing feedback because you can frame your comments around the descriptions in the rubric. Students also benefit from knowing you will use a grading rubric if you impress on them that they will be evaluated solely on how well they demonstrate knowledge acquisition and skills development tied to the learning outcomes, reducing any anxiety they may have about submitting a polished Product and helping them focus on showing their mastery.

Holistic Rubrics

A holistic rubric uses a single scale to evaluate the Product as a whole. All of the criteria being evaluated, ordinarily the learning outcomes, are grouped together into a single description at each point on the scale. Holistic rubrics are most useful when evaluating assignments or questions where the learning outcomes are interdependent and it is not necessary to examine each learning outcome one at a time. This approach can be useful for grading long essays or term papers where the learning outcomes are linked together. Using holistic rubrics can make grading quicker because you do not need to take the time to evaluate each learning outcome separately. However, in information literacy courses, it is likely more valuable to look at each learning outcome on its own, so all mentions of rubrics in the rest of this chapter and the remaining chapters in this book will presume you are using analytic rubrics.

Analytic Rubrics

An analytic rubric uses individual scales for each learning outcome being evaluated. Examining each learning outcome separately is most helpful when you are assessing students' acquisition of knowledge that is not purely factual and their performance of a complicated skill, such as conducting in-depth research. Designing and using analytic rubrics will require more of your time compared to holistic rubrics because scales with descriptions must be created for each learning outcome, and you will need to evaluate multiple learning outcomes separately as part of the grading process.

When grading with an analytic rubric, students' performance on each learning outcome can be weighted differently depending on how important that learning outcome is compared to the others. Analytic rubrics also make the process of providing detailed feedback easier because you will be able to address how well a student demonstrated mastery of each learning outcome. Your feedback can be broken down by learning outcomes so that students can quickly identify areas where they were strongest and weakest. Because the information literacy skills taught in your course will be valuable to them for the remainder of their time as a student and likely also in their career, you can suggest that students work to strengthen the areas where they were weakest, even if they can no longer improve their grade on that summative assessment.

Designing Analytic Rubrics

Establishing clear learning outcomes is a necessary precursor to designing an effective rubric. Since learning outcomes are statements of measurable or observable achievements, the descriptions you write should reflect your measurements or observations of how well the submitted Product demonstrates a student's achievement of the learning outcomes. Ideally, a student's mastery of all of the learning outcomes should be evaluated using summative assessments, whether with a single Product that covers everything taught in the course or with multiple Products spread throughout the span of the semester.

Analytic rubrics ordinarily take the form of a grid, with each learning outcome listed down the left column and the numbers for the gradation levels on the scale across the top row. A response where the student demonstrates complete mastery of all aspects of a learning outcome should be assigned the highest value on the scale, and one where little to no mastery is shown should be given the lowest value (ordinarily a value of 1). Every cell in the center should contain a description of how well a student must demonstrate mastery of the learning outcome listed at the start of that row to be given a score corresponding to the gradation level at the top of the column.

Deciding how many gradations you want to include between the highest and lowest values can be challenging. If you have taught the course before, take a look at previous students' work to get a feel for the breadth of mastery shown in the past. If the responses between are usually similar in the degree of mastery they reflect, you may need only one middle point, leaving you with a three-point scale. If there is more variety in how much mastery is demonstrated in those in-between responses, you should place two or three in-between points on your scale. If you have not taught the course before and do not have access to past students' work from when someone else taught the course, look over your students' formative assessments to get a sense of the breadth of the mastery they have shown throughout the unit or course. Also, think about how you would word the descriptions differently to reflect the differences between each point on the scale. Is there enough nuance in the way the learning outcome is measured or observed to justify having two or three in-between points?

As an example, Prof. Lee's first learning objective for the Critically Evaluating Sources unit, "Students will evaluate information sources for accuracy, authority, objectivity, purpose, currency, and appropriateness," has six associated learning outcomes. The first of these is, "Students should be able to determine the accuracy of an information source, describe their process for doing this, and justify their process and final determination convincingly." After reviewing students' submissions from past semesters, Prof. Lee determined that the responses between the top and bottom of the scale demonstrated a similar, moderately adequate degree of mastery. She decided to use an analytic rubric with a three-point scale for all the learning outcomes evaluated by the unit-end summative assessment Product. Table 6.1 contains the portion of the rubric addressing the first learning outcome,

Table 6.1   Prof. Lee's Rubric for the First Learning Outcome

	1	2	3
Accuracy	The accuracy of the information source was not determined; the process described was poorly conceived or significantly incomplete, and its justification was unconvincing or entirely missing.	The accuracy of the information source was partially determined and not well explained; the process described was rational but incomplete and inadequately justified.	The accuracy of the information source was well determined and explained convincingly; the process described was rational, thorough, and well justified.

which she shortened to "Accuracy" rather than including the full text of the learning outcome.

The description for the highest gradation summarizes what students will need to show to demonstrate full mastery of this learning outcome. The second gradation's description reflects that a response in this category shows some mastery but is lacking, and it describes in what ways a student may fall short of showing achievement of the full learning outcome. The description of the lowest gradation indicates that a student who gets this score failed to show much or any mastery. Notice that the descriptions provide detailed explanations of why a response will fall into each of the gradations and mirror the phrasing of the learning outcome rather than simply stating that a response was "poor," "good," or "excellent." Your rubric descriptions should at a minimum contain this level of detail to ensure that your grading reflects an objective assessment of the responses based on predetermined criteria.

The final step of preparing a rubric is determining how the numerical points from the scales will correspond to the scores used in grading. If you believe that all of the learning outcomes should be weighted the same, you do not need to make any adjustments to the point values. You can tally all the points a student earned and divide by the maximum number of points to get a percentage grade. If some learning outcomes are more important and should be weighted more heavily than others, you will need to determine a multiplier for each of the more important learning outcomes. For example, a learning outcome that is much more important than most of the others may merit a 3× or 2× multiplier, while a learning outcome that is somewhat more important may get a 1.5× multiplier. The point value for a learning outcome of average importance can simply carry over to your final scoring, or you can think of it as having a 1× multiplier. To determine the grade, multiply the raw point value by the multiplier, tally all the adjusted point values, and divide by the maximum adjusted point value to get a percentage grade.

It is important to test out a new rubric to make sure that it works as intended and that students end up with scores that are reflective of their achievement. If you have submissions from a past courses' Product that matches closely with the current final Product, use the rubric to evaluate those past submissions. Otherwise, once your students have submitted their final Products, you can test out the rubric on a few of those and decide whether the rubric works as intended or needs some adjustments before grading all the submissions.

Tips for Using Rubrics

For final projects or other Products that students will work on for an extended period of time, consider giving them a copy of the rubric so that they can understand what you will be looking for when grading. This way, students can self-evaluate their work to make sure they have fully demonstrated mastery before submitting it. If you are concerned that sharing your rubric with students would reveal too much about what students will be evaluated on, you can prepare an abbreviated version to provide students some idea of how they will be graded.

Once you have finished grading, you may want to compile a summary of how the class performed as a whole by tallying how many students were at each scale gradation for each learning outcome. If you find the majority of students did not demonstrate mastery of a particular learning outcome, you should consider placing more emphasis on that learning outcome the next time you teach the course. You may need to modify or create additional Content or Process learning objects so that students spend more time working on mastering that learning outcome. If you do not already use a formative assessment Product to assess students' progress with that learning outcome, you may want to add one in the future.

If your summative assessment Product contains a mix of fact-based questions and more complicated research and analysis tasks, remember that you do not need to include in your rubric questions that have clear right answers.

Research Projects

Research projects that students work on over an extended period of time can be readily adapted for differentiated instruction. These summative assessments ordinarily involve students identifying a topic early on in the semester and submitting it to the instructor for approval before researching it using the resources introduced throughout the course. Students are expected to put into practice the skills they are developing while working on the project, resulting in a final Product where they summarize their findings, explain their research strategy and reasoning for following that strategy, and describe the process they went through to implement that strategy, mentioning how they found the resources they used. In traditional instruction, this final Product is submitted as a text document, preferred by read-write learners. This summative assessment also accommodates the learning preferences of students with participative and independent learning styles.

You can differentiate research projects by offering students the option to submit their final Product or a portion of it in a format other than written text. Aural learners will benefit from being able to submit the topic proposal, summary, strategy, and process sections of the project as voice recordings. Visual learners can be accommodated by permitting students to submit presentation slide decks for the proposal and all three sections of the finished Product, or flowcharts and graphic organizers for the strategy and process sections. Collaborative and dependent learners may prefer an option to work together with a partner on strategizing before conducting their research individually.

Problem-Solving Explanations

With a problem-solving explanation summative assessment, you present students with a research task that needs to be completed—or a series of tasks—and ask them to explain every step they took to analyze the task, how they strategized to complete it, and how they identified relevant resources, conducted the research, and determined the most useful results. Ordinarily, students explain their steps in a written narrative account of their full process or in a numbered list (step one, step two, etc.), accommodating the learning preferences of read-write, participative, and independent learners. This Product can be differentiated for aural and visual learners by allowing students to use voice recordings, slide decks, or flowcharts to walk you through their steps. Visual learners may also take advantage of an option to record a screencast to demonstrate and narrate the portions where they identified resources, conducted the research, and determined the best results. Collaborative and dependent learners can be accommodated by permitting students to work with a partner on analyzing the task and strategizing an approach.

Tests and Exams

Differentiation can work for untimed, take-home tests or exams that contain some short-answer or essay questions. You can include other question types, such as multiple-choice or fill-in-the-blank, but those questions should not be differentiated. Timed, take-home, and in-class tests or exams do not lend themselves to differentiation because, given the great variation in the time it takes students to create different formats of multimedia responses, it is unfair to limit their time.

Short-answer and essay questions can be differentiated by giving students the option to submit their responses to those questions in a format other than written text. Aural learners will benefit from being allowed to submit voice recordings. Visual learners can be accommodated if you decide to accept presentation slide decks instead of written text. Slide decks can include images pertaining to the topic of the question and narration that contains a more detailed response.

Presentations

Unit-end or course-end presentations are another form of a final summative assessment. All students can prepare a presentation on researching a particular topic, such as something related to their major, and be instructed to touch on several learning outcomes as part of their explanation. Another approach is to have students design a slide deck that could be used to teach one or several of the learning outcomes in the course, accompanied by either an in-class presentation of the slide deck or embedded narration that explains the topic the way an instructor would. This Product appeals to the preferences of aural and visual learning styles. In order to accommodate read-write learners, you can allow students to submit a written script instead of presenting their slide deck in class or as narration. You may want to share the list of recommended presentation resources from Chapter Four with students, although most will already be familiar with how to use at least one presentation software application or Web-based platform.

SEVEN

Implementing Differentiated Instruction

Now that you are familiar with the components of differentiated instruction and have a variety of techniques and resources at your disposal, you are ready to put it all together to prepare differentiated courses, units, or one-shot sessions. As you work through the process of planning differentiation, creating new learning objects, and executing your plan, keep in mind the learning styles summarized in Figure 4.1 (page 47) because the two models touch on aspects of learning preferences contained in various perceptual and affective models. In this chapter, you will find suggested steps, including sample lesson plans, for implementing differentiated instruction in an information literacy course and in one-shot sessions. You will also read about Prof. Lee's experience with implementing differentiation in two units of her course and the experience of the three students who were introduced in Chapter Two.

PLANNING FOR DIFFERENTIATION IN AN INFORMATION LITERACY COURSE

Prof. Lee follows these seven suggested steps when planning for differentiating her first-year information literacy course:

Suggested Steps for Planning Differentiated Instruction in a Course

1. Decide whether to differentiate the entire course or just some units.
2. Determine the course objectives and learning outcomes.

3. Decide whether to administer a preassessment. Will you use the results of the preassessment to decide how to differentiate Content, Process, and Product?

4. Plan how to differentiate Content. Create new Content learning objects, if needed.

5. Plan how to differentiate Process. Create new Process learning objects, if needed.

6. Plan how to differentiate Product. Will you use formative assessments? Create new Product learning objects, if needed. Create answer keys for formative assessments and rubrics for summative assessments.

7. Create lesson plans for class sessions.

1. Decide Whether to Differentiate the Entire Course or Just Some Units

Because of the flexibility of differentiated instruction, you do not need to differentiate an entire course and can choose to apply the approach in only one or a few units, as discussed in Chapter Three. Differentiating a few, select units allows you to test out how well differentiation works for you and your students and can help you learn how much work is involved in the creation of new learning objects using the techniques and tools presented in Chapters Four, Five, and Six. As mentioned in Chapter One, Prof. Lee decided to differentiate the Search Strategies and Critically Evaluating Sources units of the course, as well as the course-end project, as her first foray into differentiated instruction. She also decided to keep the weighting of the graded portions of the course the same as the previous several times she has taught it: 25% for a multiple-choice midterm, 55% for the course-end project, and 20% for completion of homework assignments. Because the two differentiated units will not contain any homework assignments, active participation in the Process learning objects will be counted instead.

2. Determine the Course Objectives and Learning Outcomes

In Chapter Three, you learned that the first step in preparing for differentiation is to create specific course objectives and learning outcomes. Although Prof. Lee decided to wait until after the preassessment to begin preparing the learning objects for the two differentiated units, as part of her course preparation she identified the course objectives and learning outcomes for every unit and wrote them into the syllabus. The course objective for the Search Strategies unit is, "Students will learn how to find information effectively and efficiently by using a variety of search strategies and appreciate the benefits of each strategy." The associated learning outcomes are:

- Students should be able to devise an effective and efficient strategy to search for, identify, and access information relevant to an information need.
- Students should be able to describe the benefits and drawbacks of each search strategy learned.

The course objectives for the Critically Evaluating Sources unit are:

1. Students will evaluate information sources for accuracy, authority, objectivity, purpose, currency, and appropriateness.
2. Students will critically reflect on the political, economic, and social frameworks surrounding the production and dissemination of the sources.

The associated learning outcomes are:

- Students should be able to:
  - Determine the accuracy of an information source, describe their process for doing this, and justify their process and final determination convincingly.
  - Examine the expertise and credibility of the author of an information source in the context of how the information will be used, determine whether the author's expertise and credibility are sufficient to lend authority to the source, describe their process for making this determination, and justify their process and final determination convincingly.
  - Assess an information source's objectivity by identifying its facts, opinions, point of view, and bias; determine whether a source is sufficiently objective to be useful for its intended purpose; describe the process for making this determination; and justify their process and final determination convincingly.
  - Determine the purpose for an information source and whether it is useful for the intended purpose, describe their process for making this determination, and justify their process and final determination convincingly.

- Determine whether a source is sufficiently current to be useful for its intended purpose, describe their process for making this determination, and justify their process and final determination convincingly.
- Assess whether an information source is appropriate for its intended purpose, describe their assessment process, and justify their process and final assessment convincingly.
- Explain how and why some individuals or groups of individuals may be underrepresented or systematically marginalized within the systems that produce and disseminate information.
- Recognize and describe issues of access or lack of access to information sources.
- Describe how distinct communities may recognize different types of authority.

3. Decide Whether to Administer a Preassessment

Chapter Three discusses the usefulness of administering a preassessment for determining students' readiness, revealing their interests, and investigating their learning styles. For many years, Prof. Lee has administered a preassessment to students to find out about their familiarity with the information literacy topics covered in the course and their past experience with developing relevant skills. For this course, she adds three questions to the end of the preassessment questionnaire asking about students' career and personal interests, learning preferences, and preference for some of the differentiated learning objects she is considering using.

4. Plan How to Differentiate Content

After the first class session, Prof. Lee reviews the students' completed preassessments and uses their responses to the three new questions to help plan the Content, Process, and formative assessment Product learning objects for the two differentiated units. Among the Content choices, the most popular options were readings and streaming videos instead of lectures. She decides to offer both of these Content options to students. The information contained in the readings will be the same as the information in the video screencasts, so students will need to engage only with one.

Textbooks and Other Readings

Concise reading assignments accommodate the learning preferences of read-write and independent learning styles. In past courses, Prof. Lee assigned students one or two chapters of the course textbook to read before class and then lectured during class sessions. However, the information in the textbook readings did not contain some of the information she introduced in class and vice versa. In order to close this gap for the differentiated units' readings, Prof. Lee writes a document for each unit, based off her past lecture notes, to serve as an additional reading assignment. During this process, she makes sure that neither the textbook readings nor the new documents contain any information that is not relevant to one of the learning outcomes for that unit.

Screencast Lectures and Mini-Lessons

Rather than create one long screencast video for each unit, Prof. Lee plans out a series of mini-lessons, with each one focusing on the material related to one of the course objectives and its associated learning outcomes. She anticipates that this approach will accommodate the learning preferences of aural, visual, and independent learners, in addition to students with short attention spans. She prepares a screencast script for each mini-lesson, drawing together the information from the textbook, the new documents, and her past lecture notes. For several years, she has used PowerPoint slide decks during her lectures. The most recent slide decks for the Search Strategies and Critically Evaluating Sources lectures serve as the starting place for Prof. Lee's screencast slides. She uses the Creative Commons Web site's search to find images for her slides and adds a text box at the bottom of each slide where she puts the attribution for the images in a small font size. She notices that some of the past slides contain a substantial amount of text and reduces how much text appears on those slides, while making sure that all of that information is contained in the script for that mini-lesson.

Once the scripts and slide decks are finished, Prof. Lee begins preparing to record the screencasts. She borrows a Blue Yeti USB microphone from the school's audiovisual department to record the narration. Setting up the microphone takes her a couple of minutes. Because she wants to record while sitting at her desk, she puts some books under the microphone so it is at about the same height as her mouth. She places the microphone away from her mouth by about the width of two fists. Within 20 minutes of beginning to set up the microphone, she has recorded a few audio samples in QuickTime Player on her Mac to test out the audio quality and is ready to move on to learning to use the free version of ActivePresenter screencasting software.

Prof. Lee spends an hour learning how to record and edit with ActivePresenter and how to use some of the cursor effects. She then records the Search Strategies mini-lesson, displaying the PowerPoint slides in full screen mode on her computer while reading through the script in a natural tone to narrate the lesson. Every time she stumbles on her words or makes some other mistake while speaking, she snaps her fingers close to the microphone to create a spike on the audio track's waveform in ActivePresenter to mark the point right after where she needs to edit out the mistake, then repeats that portion of the script and continues on with the recording. Once she is done recording, she plays back the file, quickly cuts out the mistakes she marked, but does not edit out every "um" or other filler word. She then records and edits the other two mini-lessons, with each video ending up being about 12 to 15 minutes in length.

Content Distribution via a Learning Management System

When Prof. Lee set up her course site in the school's learning management system, she set up empty unit modules for the two differentiated units. She creates a Content folder in each of the modules and uploads the documents there. She uploads the mini-lesson videos to the library's YouTube account and sets them as unlisted so that they can be accessed only by using the exact URL for each video. The unlisted videos do not appear in the listing of the library's videos or in search engine results, including YouTube's internal search. Prof. Lee then sets up a class preparation assignment in each unit's module, where she explains that students have the choice of either reading the textbook and document or watching the streaming videos for that unit.

5. Plan How to Differentiate Process

For Prof. Lee, planning how to differentiate the learning objects that students will use to make sense of what they are learning turns out to be the most challenging part of adopting differentiated instruction. She initially intends to dedicate the entirety of each 60-minute class session for the two differentiated units to Process and knows that this will require her to create several new learning objects. She wants to balance the offering of Process activities so that many different learning styles are accommodated. The Search Strategies unit has one class session, and the Critically Evaluating Sources unit has two.

Review and Discussion

Because Prof. Lee is accustomed to lecturing during class, the idea of starting class immediately with an active learning exercise, without any discussion of the material contained in the Content, seems odd to her. In order to ease into active learning, she decides that each class session will begin with a 10-minute Review and Discussion, as described in Chapter Five, so that students can spend some time on synthesizing the material before moving on to in-class exercises. The review portion of this activity accommodates the learning preference of visual, aural, and dependent learners while the discussion is most appealing to aural, participative, and collaborative learners. For each class session, she prepares two slides in PowerPoint, with the first containing an outline of the topics covered in the Content for that unit. She plans to display the slide at the start of class and ask students whether they have any questions about each point in the outline, moving through it from top to bottom. She will have the slide decks she used for the screencasts on a flash drive, ready to open if she needs to refer to any particular slides while answering questions. For the second slide of each session, she creates three review questions that she will use to engage the class in a discussion, if any time remains in the first 10 minutes of class.

Replacing Demonstrations

As part of her lecture on search strategies in past semesters, Prof. Lee conducted brief in-class demonstrations of how to use the college's library catalog and aggregated search platform, conduct field searches in databases (using Gale's Academic OneFile as an example), and search with Google Scholar. With differentiated instruction, instead of demonstrating these research tools in class, she finds already existing video demonstrations and tutorials for students to watch before class. The library has a series of videos on searching its catalog and aggregated platform that, combined, run about nine minutes. Prof. Lee finds a video on YouTube created by another academic library on how to use Google Scholar that does a thorough job of explaining the basic and advanced search options in about six minutes. Gale's Web site contains many tutorial videos, including four on using the InfoTrac search interface that is used by Academic OneFile, and Prof. Lee assigns five videos that run a total of 15 minutes. Prof. Lee believes that all the videos do an equivalent job of demonstrating the tools and search strategies compared to what she ordinarily does in class. Demonstrations appeal to visual, aural, participative, collaborative, and dependent learners.

Comparing Resources and Results

For about 45 minutes of the Search Strategies class session, as well as the first Critically Evaluating Sources class, Prof. Lee plans to have students work in small groups on Comparing Resources and Results, a Process active learning exercise that accommodates the learning needs of visual, aural, read-write, kinesthetic, participative, collaborative, competitive, dependent, and independent learners. For the Search Strategies class, she will create groups of three or four students with the same learning style, based on their preassessment responses, their 10-minute meetings with her, and her observations of them up to that point in the semester. She prepares a PowerPoint slide that shows the groupings. Prof. Lee picks three topics to research related to the professional and personal interests that students revealed on their preassessment—the use of checklists in hospitals to improve the quality of patient care; the impact of voter registration laws on suppressing the vote of marginalized groups; and the benefit and drawbacks of the computerized Graduate Record Examinations (GRE) compared to the paper version.

For the first round of the exercise, each student will be assigned one of the three search tools demonstrated in the videos to use to find scholarly articles on the first subject. The students will practice Boolean searching in the library's aggregated search platform, keyword searching in Google Scholar, and subject searching with a controlled vocabulary in Academic OneFile. Students will research for up to 10 minutes and discuss their results and impressions of the search tool with their group for up to five minutes. Then each student will pick a different search tool and repeat the research and discussion process for that topic. Similarly, each student will repeat the process for the third topic with the remaining search tool. Students will need to save their search results to use in the first Critically Evaluating Sources class session. Prof. Lee does not design a differentiated alternative for this exercise, so all students will need to participate in the small-group activity.

For the first Critically Evaluating Sources class session, students will have the option of doing the exercise on their own, instead of in a small group, in order to accommodate independent learners. Those students who opt to work in a small group will organize themselves into groups of three with students sitting near them in class, so as to not create too much disruption and delay while rearranging their desks. Prof. Lee designs the exercise to build on the same three topics and sets of search results as the Search Strategies small-group work. In the first round, each group will have 10 minutes to choose a relatively short article from the first topic's search results to individually skim and evaluate, using the criteria and process discussed in the readings and videos for that unit. The groups will then discuss their evaluations of that article for five minutes. The same process will be repeated for the second and third topics. The students who choose to work on their own will choose an article and evaluate it but will not discuss their evaluations.

Think-Pair-Share

For the second Critically Evaluating Sources class session, Prof. Lee plans to allocate 25 minutes to a Think-Pair-Share activity after the Review and Discussion. This activity appeals to the learning preferences of aural, kinesthetic, participative, collaborative, and dependent students. The prompt for the activity is, "Come up with one way that the issue of access to information for members of marginalized groups could be addressed. Be creative!" Students will have three minutes to think of an idea and write it down. Then they will pair up to talk about their ideas for seven minutes. Afterward, a 15-minute class discussion will take place where each pair of students shares one person's idea with the whole class and summarizes the discussion they had about that idea. Other students and Prof. Lee can chime in with their thoughts and suggestions about each idea presented.

Preparing Study Materials

Prof. Lee plans to dedicate the time remaining after the Think-Pair-Share activity in the second Critically Evaluating Sources class session to the final Process activity, Preparing Study Materials, because the midterm will occur the week after the session. This activity appeals to the learning preferences of visual, read-write, kinesthetic, participative, collaborative, and dependent learners. She prepares a PowerPoint presentation about several different study techniques that appeal to different learning styles and plans to spend up to 10 minutes presenting these ideas to the class. Students will then have about 25 minutes to work in groups of three or four to briefly discuss which of the techniques they already use or would like to try. The group will then choose one technique to work on together and will spend the rest of the class period beginning to create study materials for the unit using that technique.

6. Plan How to Differentiate Product

Prof. Lee has not used formative assessment Products before in her course and would like to include them in the differentiated units. For the course-end summative assessment, she plans to have students do a Research Project, with differentiated options for the format that students can use.

Practice Quiz

There are a series of review and analysis questions at the end of each textbook chapter that she has encouraged students in past courses to read and think about, but she has never required them to submit answers. Prof. Lee writes similar questions for the end of each document and decides to require all students to submit answers for both the textbook and document questions via the school's learning management system quiz tool to serve as an ungraded, formative assessment. Each unit's practice quiz is designed as a series of short-answer questions where she fills in the chapter and question number in the area where the quiz tool expects instructors to write the question text rather than retyping the text from the chapter or document. She writes answers for each question within the quiz tool and selects the setting to display the answers once students submit the quiz so that they can receive immediate feedback. Recognizing that it may be more valuable to students to complete the quiz at the end of a unit, after they have completed the Process active learning exercises and have had time to make sense of the material, she sets the deadline for each quiz to four days after the last class session of the respective unit.

Minute Papers

The idea of having students write Minute Papers as an end-of-class summary is also intriguing to Prof. Lee, who plans to use them in the Search Strategies class session and the first Critically Evaluating Sources class. This formative assessment activity provides students an opportunity to quickly reflect on what they have learned and what remains unclear to them. Prof. Lee creates a PowerPoint slide with the two prompt questions: "What is the most important thing you learned about the topic(s) covered in today's class?" and "What is the muddiest point left unanswered?" She plans to end the Comparing Resources and Results exercise five minutes before class is over so that students can write their Minute Papers and then turn them in as they leave the classroom. She intends to address any points that several students find muddy in an e-mail to the whole class within a day or two of the class session, serving as the feedback for this formative assessment.

Research Project

The last learning object left for Prof. Lee to plan is the course-end Research Project, one of two summative assessment Products in the course. While the other summative assessment, the multiple-choice midterm, cannot be differentiated, Prof. Lee plans to offer differentiated options for all aspects of the Research Project. There are four components to the summative assessment: a proposal due around the middle of the semester and the final submission's strategy, process, and summary of findings sections.

Prof. Lee plans to distribute the Research Project instructions at the beginning of the class session that takes place two days after the midterm, in week eight of the semester. One week later, students will need to submit a research proposal where they identify the topic they will be researching, including the specific question that they would address if they were actually writing a term paper using the resources they find. Ordinarily, students would submit the proposal as a typed document. Prof. Lee rewrites the instructions to also allow students to submit the proposal as a voice recording or presentation slide deck in order to accommodate aural and visual learners.

For the Research Project submission, students must explain their research strategy and reasoning for following that strategy, describe the process they went through to implement that strategy, and summarize their findings. Prof. Lee rewrites the instructions to permit students to submit the strategy and process sections as audio recordings, slide decks, flowcharts, or graphic organizers. Portions of the summary of findings can also be submitted as audio recordings or slide decks. Prof. Lee has never allowed any student collaboration on summative assessments before in her course but decides to offer students the option to work together with a partner on strategizing before conducting their research individually in order to accommodate collaborative and dependent learners. Any students who choose this option will need to identify the partner in the strategy section of the submission.

Because Prof. Lee will accept Research Project submissions in a variety of different formats, it is critical that she use a grading rubric to evaluate how well students demonstrated their mastery of the learning outcomes, regardless of the format. She designs an analytic rubric to use when reviewing the final submissions, a sample of which is shown in Table 6.1 in Chapter Six (page 106). She will rely on the rubric not only for grading but for constructing the feedback she will give each student by basing her comments on the students' demonstration of mastery, as detailed in the rubric. Instead of sharing the rubric with students in advance, she provides substantial detail in the instructions so that students understand what they will be expected to demonstrate in each section, as shown in the following excerpt from the instructions:

Research Proposal: Identify a research topic that you might write about in a term paper, including the specific question that you would address. The proposal can be submitted as either a text document, a slide deck, or an audio recording in MP3 or M4A format. Do not begin researching until your topic has been approved by me.

Strategy: Before conducting any research, plan out a strategy for how you will search for, identify, and access information relevant to your topic. Describe your strategy and reasoning for following that strategy in the first section of your final submission, including the benefits and draw-backs of each search technique you decide to use. You can collaborate with one classmate on this section to discuss strategy ideas. If you collaborate, identify that person at the beginning. This section can be submitted as either written text, an audio recording, a slide deck, flow-charts, or a graphic organizer.

Process: Describe the process of implementing your strategy and narrow-ing down the search results to the sources you will use. Mention all the research tools you use and how effective they were for helping you find resources relevant to your research question. Provide sufficient details so that I am able to recreate your research process, if needed. Do not describe the resources you select to rely on in your hypothetical term paper; you will do this in the next section. This section can be submitted as either a text document, an audio recording, a slide deck, flowcharts, or a graphic organizer.

Summary of Findings: Choose at least five, and no more than eight, resources from your search results that you would rely on. Provide an MLA-style citation for each resource in a written document. Then explain why you chose each resource and give an evaluation of its accuracy, authority, objectivity, purpose, currency, and appropriateness. The explanations and evaluations can be submitted within the text document that con-tains the citations, or as audio recordings or slide decks.

For the first resource you include, explain the process you went through to evaluate it and why you came up with each determination for the multiple criteria. This can be submitted as text, an audio record-ing, or slide deck. Then summarize how the resources address your question, either in no more than six text paragraphs or in an equivalent-length audio recording or slide deck.

Deadlines and Submission Process: The research proposal is due at the end of week 9, and all three sections of the project are due at the end of week 15. Everything should be submitted in the Research Project mod-ule of the learning management system, either as file attachments or URLs to an online version of that portion.

Using the Learning Outcomes: The learning outcomes in the syllabus describe what you are expected to learn in this course. For the units that are related to this project, use the learning outcomes as your guide for what knowledge and skills I will be looking for you to demonstrate in your submission.

7. Create Lesson Plans for Class Sessions

Lesson plans are a helpful tool to ensure that you manage the face-to-face time with your students well and keep your class sessions focused on the course objectives and associated learning outcomes. At a minimum, your lesson plan should include a schedule of how you will allocate classroom time that you can refer to throughout the session so that you do not run out of time. Although there may be times when you decide to be flexible with the schedule for a session, such as when students are particularly engaged in a class discussion and you do not want to cut it off prematurely to move onto the next planned activity, you should aim to adhere to the predetermined schedule to avoid forgoing any of the activities you thought were valuable enough to include in the schedule. You should also consider including the course objectives, learning outcomes, summary of Content choices, and a listing of any other work students are expected to do before or after class, as part of your lesson plan so that you can quickly refer to them throughout the class session.

Now that Prof. Lee has planned the Content, Process, and Product learning objects for the two differentiated units, she prepares the lesson plans for the three class sessions, shown in Figures 7.1–7.3.

Solicit Feedback from Students

When you have completed the differentiated course or units, you should solicit feedback from students about their learning experience. Student feedback can assist you with identifying any changes that may be needed to improve your differentiated instruction. Be prepared for negative feedback from some students who simply did not like the approach because it was different from what they are accustomed to. You should weigh this type of feedback and any other negative feedback against your goal of helping students of varied readiness, interest, and learning styles to succeed.

Prof. Lee asks students to answer these three questions about their experience with differentiated instruction via an anonymous Google Form:

1. What did you like about the differentiated units and Research Project, and why?
2. What did you not like about them, and why?
3. What changes do you suggest for the differentiated units and Research Project?

Search Strategies Lesson Plan

Course Objective: Students will learn how to find information effectively and efficiently by using a variety of search strategies and appreciate the benefits of each strategy.

Learning Outcomes: Students should be able to...
- devise an effective and efficient strategy to search for, identify, and access information relevant to an information need.
- describe the benefits and drawbacks of each search technique learned.

Content: Choice between 1) Readings (textbook chapter 3 and Search Strategies document) or 2) One mini-lesson YouTube video

Process, pre-class: Library videos on using the online catalog and aggregated search tool; YouTube video on basic and advanced searching in Google Scholar; four Gale videos on using the InfoTrac interface

Schedule

Time	Activity (type)
0-10	Review and Discussion (Process – whole group)
10-55	Comparing Resources and Results (Process – small groups)
55-60	Minute Paper (Product – formative assessment)

Product, post-class: Practice quiz (formative assessment)

Figure 7.1 Search Strategies Lesson Plan

EXECUTING THE DIFFERENTIATION PLAN

Introducing Differentiation

Before administering the preassessment on the first day of class, Prof. Lee tells the students that she will be using differentiated instruction in two units in the course and explains the approach and its benefits. She shares with them her reasons for adopting the approach, focusing on her observations about learning styles and the impact of students' culture on how they learn. She also conveys that she trusts them to take greater responsibility for their learning. She explains how she will use the students' responses to the final three questions of the preassessment to help her plan the

---

Critically Evaluating Sources Class 1 Lesson Plan

Course Objective: Students will evaluate information sources for accuracy, authority, objectivity, purpose, currency, and appropriateness.

Learning Outcomes: Students should be able to...
- determine the accuracy of an information source, describe their process for doing this, and justify their process and final determination convincingly.
- examine the expertise and credibility of the author of an information source in the context of how the information will be used, determine if the author's expertise and credibility is sufficient to lend authority to the source, describe their process for making this determination, and justify their process and final determination convincingly.
- assess an information source's objectivity by identifying its facts, opinions, point of view, and bias; determine whether a source is sufficiently objective to be useful for its intended purpose; describe the process for making this determination; and justify their process and final determination convincingly.
- determine the purpose for an information source and whether it is useful for the intended purpose, describe their process for making this determination, and justify their process and final determination convincingly.
- determine whether a source is sufficiently current to be useful for its intended purpose, describe their process for making this determination, and justify their process and final determination convincingly.
- assess whether an information source is appropriate for its intended purpose, describe their assessment process, and justify their process and final assessment convincingly.

Content: Choice between 1) Readings (textbook chapter 4 and Critically Evaluating Sources document) or 2) Two mini-lesson YouTube videos

---

Schedule

Time	Activity (type)
0-10	Review and Discussion (Process – whole group)
10-55	Comparing Resources and Results (Process – small groups or individually)
55-60	Minute Paper (Product – formative assessment)

Figure 7.2 Critically Evaluating Sources Class 1 Lesson Plan

Critically Evaluating Sources Class 2 Lesson Plan

Course Objective: Students will critically reflect on the political, economic, and social frameworks surrounding the production and dissemination of the sources.

Learning Outcomes: Students should be able to...
- explain how and why some individuals or groups of individuals may be underrepresented or systematically marginalized within the systems that produce and disseminate information.
- recognize and describe issues of access or lack of access to information sources.
- describe how distinct communities may recognize different types of authority.

Content: Choice between 1) Readings (textbook chapter 4 and Critically Evaluating Sources document) or 2) Two mini-lesson YouTube videos

---

Schedule

Time	Activity (type)
0-10	Review and Discussion (Process – whole group)
10-35	Think-Pair-Share (Process – small groups)
35-60	Preparing Study Materials (Process – small groups or individually)

Product, post-class: Practice quiz (formative assessment)

Figure 7.3 Critically Evaluating Sources Class 2 Lesson Plan

differentiated units. She acknowledges that many students may not be familiar with differentiation and active learning and asks that they keep an open mind about the approach and the techniques to be used in those units. Overall, the introduction of differentiation is primarily student focused, with Prof. Lee emphasizing several times the benefits she hopes students will experience from the changes.

The Differentiated Units

The availability of the Content options for both differentiated units is announced by Prof. Lee via e-mail two weeks before the Search Strategies class session and is also posted in the learning management system. On the day of that session, only a few students raise questions during the Review and Discussion. One student asks several questions that reveal his confusion with how to use field searching in Academic OneFile. After the third question, Prof. Lee suggests that she work with him and his group during the Comparing Resources and Results activity to go through the first part together in Academic OneFile. Prof. Lee is able to hold a discussion about the first two review questions before the 10 minutes are over.

The students quickly arrange themselves into their groups for the Comparing Resources and Results activity while Prof. Lee explains how it will work and distributes a handout with instructions and the three topics to research. Once the groups have begun the exercise, Prof. Lee joins the group with the student who had several questions and works with them on researching the first topic together in Academic OneFile. Afterward, she walks around the room, stops to check how every group is progressing, and finds that at least one person in nearly every group asks her for clarification on how to use one of the three search tools that are part of the exercise. Within a few minutes, students are raising their hands or calling out to her to get her attention because they have questions. For the remainder of the time allotted for the activity, Prof. Lee hops from one group to another to answer questions.

When five minutes of class time remain, Prof. Lee ends the Comparing Resources and Results activity and explains to students how the Minute Papers will work. She displays a slide with the two prompt questions on the projection screen, and students spend the remaining time handwriting or typing their answers. She was planning on everyone handwriting their responses, but some students asked it if would be okay to e-mail them to her, and she agreed.

Prof. Lee is pleased with how the first differentiated class session turned out. Nearly every student seemed to have completed one of the Content options and watched the demonstration videos, although she observed one student asking her groupmates many questions about how to use the three search tools, making Prof. Lee wonder if the student had not watched the videos. On the Minute Papers, most students wrote that the muddiest point was not knowing when to use one search tool over another. In an e-mail follow-up, Prof. Lee explains that it is best to use more than one search tool when available, a point that was also made in the Content, and answers the other muddiest points that students wrote. She also reminds them that they need to complete the Practice Quiz formative assessment within four days.

During the first Critically Evaluating Sources class session, many students raise questions in the Review and Discussion about how to evaluate sources on the six criteria introduced in the Content. Rather than directly answering every question and moving on to the next, Prof. Lee takes the opportunity to have a brief discussion with the class about some of the students' questions. Addressing all the questions takes 15 minutes, five more minutes than allocated, and no time is available to have a discussion about any of the review questions before beginning the Comparing Resources and Results activity. Four students opt to complete the activity individually, while the rest work in groups. Prof. Lee is even busier than during the Search Strategies activity, answering questions from the groups and the four students working on their own. As soon as she is finished with one group or individual, another student's hand goes up in the air. Sometimes one or two groups are waiting on her to finish with another group, although those who are waiting continue to work on the exercise. With three minutes left in the class period, Prof. Lee asks students to complete a Minute Paper and displays the slide with the two prompts.

After class, Prof. Lee makes a note on her lesson plan that, in future courses, she should allocate more time to the Review and Discussion for this session in case students have as many questions as the class did that day. She reviews the Minute Papers and notices that a few of the muddiest points are identified by more than one student but that most of the points raised are unique to a single student. She sends an e-mail addressing the muddiest points within a few hours of class ending.

In the final differentiated class session, the second of the Critically Evaluating Sources unit, the Review and Discussion goes smoothly, and Prof. Lee and the class have time to discuss the three review questions she wrote within the 10 minutes allotted. Prof. Lee then introduces the Think-Pair-Share activity to the class and gives students three minutes to write a response before pairing up with a classmate to discuss their responses for seven minutes. During the 15-minute period where students share one idea from each pair, the discussion is lively, with students responding positively to their peers' ideas and offering supportive suggestions.

Prof. Lee then explains the Preparing Study Materials activity and spends 10 minutes presenting a variety of different techniques for the students to consider. When it is time to divide into groups or work individually, two students choose to work alone. While walking around the room and checking on the groups and individual students, Prof. Lee is pleased to learn that several students who do not have a read-write learning style are already using some of the study techniques that she mentioned. Many students who were not familiar with any of the techniques are eager to try some of them out when studying for the midterm. As class ends, Prof. Lee reminds the students to complete the Practice Quiz for the unit within four days.

The Research Project Summative Assessment

When Prof. Lee distributes the instructions for the Research Project, she explains the differentiated options and lets the class know that they should e-mail her or visit her during office hours if they have any questions about the options. Within a few days of receiving the instructions, seven students out of 25 ask questions about the differentiated options. Two students submit their proposals as audio recordings, one student turns in a PowerPoint slide deck, and the others all submit text documents. The same two students who submitted audio recordings for their proposal also use them as part of their final submissions, although one of those students decides to write the whole summary of findings. One student submits a mix of slide decks and flowcharts for the final submission, and three submit flowcharts for one or two sections.

Using a rubric makes the process of grading the final submissions straightforward and methodical for Prof. Lee. When grading the portions where students submitted audio recordings, she needs to pause frequently to assess each element covered in the audio against the rubric. Grading the slide decks and flowcharts is very similar to grading the text documents. She steps through the slides and compares the information provided in each one against the relevant part of the rubric. On the whole, Prof. Lee finds that grading the differentiated options takes her only slightly more time than grading the text documents.

THE THREE STUDENTS' EXPERIENCES

Because differentiated instruction is a student-centered teaching approach, the real value of implementing it comes to light when examining the students' experience with differentiation. As mentioned in Chapter One, Prof. Lee decided to try differentiating two units because she wanted to do more to accommodate students with various learning styles but did not want to disadvantage those students who do well on traditional written assignments and thought that giving students differentiated choices could be the solution. Now, you will learn how differentiation impacted the learning experiences of the students you were introduced to in Chapter Two and whether they benefited from having choices in Content, Process, and Product.

Henry

Henry expressed enthusiasm for differentiated instruction at the beginning of the semester, and he looks forward to the start of the first differentiated unit on Search Strategies. He watches the mini-lesson YouTube video the weekend before the class session, pausing repeatedly to take notes. After watching it once and taking notes, he decides to rewatch it to see whether he missed anything important in his notes. While watching the video tutorials for the three search tools, he recreates all the steps in his Web browser and pauses to spend additional time exploring the features. He finds the tutorials incredibly helpful and likes that he can take his time with each video, which he would not be able to do if he were trying to follow along with a live demonstration in class.

During the Review and Discussion portion of the class session, Henry is the first to chime in on the first review question presented by Prof. Lee. He appreciates that she spent only a brief time reviewing the material from the video so that the class could have a few minutes to discuss some questions that get them thinking more critically about the topic. Once the students arrange themselves into their preassigned groups and begin working on the Comparing Resources and Results activity, he gets into a good flow with his groupmates and feels that they work well together. He has always liked group work because he can share his ideas with other students and talk with them about what they are learning. As someone who spends a good amount of time with his extended family in the local area, before making important decisions, Henry prefers talking with his relatives and getting their input, and this preference extends into his academic life. He finds that some of his groupmates are just as engaged in the activity as he is and that they have insights into the search tools that he would not have come up with on his own. Henry also likes knowing that Prof. Lee is available to answer their questions as they arise, even though the group ends up having only one question for her.

Henry is familiar with the Minute Paper format because a few of his high school teachers used the activity at the end of class periods, and he is happy to hear that they are writing one at the end of this session. He opts to e-mail his Minute Paper to Prof. Lee and is surprised by how quickly she sends the class an e-mail follow-up addressing some of the muddiest points, including his. When he gets home that evening, he decides to complete the Practice Quiz, even though he has four days to do it. He finds the quiz questions challenging but fair, and he appreciates that the quiz tool in the learning management system corrects his quiz automatically and, for the questions he got wrong, shows him the right answer immediately.

Henry is similarly pleased with the way things go during the first Critically Evaluating Sources class session. He and his groupmates from the Search Strategies session worked so well together that they decide to also collaborate on the Comparing Resources and Results activity in this session, and it goes just as well. They end up having more questions for Prof. Lee this time around, as does every group, but he is understanding about the need to be patient until Prof. Lee can get to them. They continue working while they wait, moving on to the next round of evaluations until Prof. Lee has time to answer their questions. Henry finds Prof. Lee's feedback on the students' Minute Papers especially helpful for this lesson because many of the points that are muddy to him are also muddy to his classmates, and the feedback addresses them clearly.

The Think-Pair-Share activity in the last differentiated class session is new to Henry. He pairs up with one of his friends who happens to be sitting next to him and enjoys chatting about their ideas for improving access to information for members of marginalized groups. They decide to share Henry's idea with the class during the discussion portion, where some classmates share positive feedback and creative suggestions. Henry also ends up commenting on two of the ideas presented by the other pairs and finds the activity to be thought provoking and engaging.

Of all the in-class activities that Prof. Lee plans for the differentiated sessions, Henry finds the Preparing Study Materials exercise to be most beneficial to him. He has never heard of graphic organizers and thinks that the approach may be useful for him to organize the information he is learning in a way that enables him to see the associations among different topics all at once. He finds two other students who are interested in creating a graphic organizer for the material in the Critically Evaluating Sources unit, and, together, they the use Visme to begin creating a mind map. When the class session is almost over, Henry suggests they get together later that week to finish their mind map, and they both agree.

For the Research Project, Henry is happy to see that Prof. Lee includes an option to submit slide decks, flowcharts, and graphic organizers for certain portions. He uses a PowerPoint presentation for his proposal of researching the topic of time/wage theft in nursing, a situation where nurses often work through their breaks and are not paid by their employers for that time. For the final submission, he does not collaborate with a classmate on strategy and turns in flowcharts for both the strategy and process sections. Henry creates rough first drafts of the flowcharts while he is working on the project, instead of putting them together at the end of the process, because they help him think through the steps he is planning and executing. When conducting the research, he walks through his planned strategy step by step, which he finds easy to do because it is neatly laid out as a flowchart. He believes that this approach works much better for him than writing out a strategy because it is easy to refer back to the flowchart and find his place, instead of skimming a written strategy to determine what to do next. He considers preparing a slide deck for part of the findings section but decides to write out the whole section.

Henry's anonymous feedback at the end of the semester about the differentiated units and Research Project is entirely positive. He praises Prof. Lee for the options she gave for the Content, Process, and Product. His suggestion for changes is to differentiate more of the course because he felt that he understood the material in the differentiated units better than in the other units and believes future students can benefit from more differentiation.

Janet

Janet is skeptical of how well differentiated instruction will work for her but tries to keep an open mind going into the Search Strategies unit. She is glad to see that Prof. Lee offers readings as one of the Content options. She finds the search tools' tutorial videos convenient because she prefers that instructors not spend time in class conducting demonstrations. While watching the videos, she reproduces the steps in her Web browser and runs some additional searches using the keyword "cybersecurity" to see what resources the library has in its collection and what else has been published and added to Google Scholar.

The Review and Discussion portion of the Search Strategies class session seems to Janet like an efficient use of time because Prof. Lee does not repeat the material that is in the readings. She likes that the class gets some time to discuss the review questions together, and she participates in the discussion for one of the questions. When Prof. Lee introduces the Comparing Resources and Results activity, Janet is glad to hear that it is ungraded because she does not know her groupmates and does not have to be concerned that their work will impact her grade. She enjoys getting to discuss the search tools and results with two classmates and being able to share her impressions of how useful the tools are.

The activity from the Search Strategies class that Janet likes best is the Minute Paper. She has never completed one before but appreciates that Prof. Lee is taking the time to find out what they think is the most important thing they learned and also what point is muddiest, so that she can address the muddy points in a follow-up e-mail. Janet does not recall a time when an instructor made an effort to assess students' progress while they were in the process of learning something and is pleased that Prof. Lee is making such an effort. Similarly, she thinks the Practice Quiz is a great addition because she likes opportunities where she can check her understanding of what she is learning and appreciates the immediate feedback.

At the beginning of the first Critically Evaluating Sources class session, Janet is surprised that so many students are asking questions because she did not have any difficulty understanding the material in the readings. She likes that Prof. Lee turns the questions into a discussion so that everyone can participate in addressing the questions. For the Comparing Resources and Results activity, Janet decides to work on her own and is glad that she has the option to do so. When Prof. Lee announces near the end of the class that they will be doing another Minute Paper, Janet hopes that this will continue throughout the rest of the semester because it was rather helpful to her the first time it was done.

In the final differentiated class session, Janet again participates in the Review and Discussion portion at the beginning of the session. She finds Think-Pair-Share to be an interesting activity and likes hearing and getting to comment on her classmates' ideas during the group discussion portion. When Prof. Lee begins presenting different techniques for Preparing Study Materials, Janet takes extensive notes because she wants to try out all of the suggestions to see if any work well for her. Once it is time for students to try creating their own study materials, Janet starts creating a hand-drawn mind map graphic organizer on her own for the Critically Evaluating Sources topics. She spends the 25 minutes remaining in class working on the mindmap and decides that she will try studying with it that evening. Although she learns that using a mind map is not an effective way for her to study, she is pleased that Prof. Lee is invested enough in the students' learning to give them time to try out something new to help them study.

Janet decides to write the Research Project proposal and all the sections, so she does not take advantage of any of the differentiated options. In her feedback about the differentiated units, she expresses that she generally liked the approach because she had options to learn the material from readings and write the final project, which she prefers. She shares that she found the activities to be interesting and more beneficial than listening to an in-class lecture. She liked getting to put the material into practice while having Prof. Lee available to answer questions. Janet's feedback about the formative assessments is quite positive because she appreciated getting the opportunity to test her understanding on the Practice Quizzes and let Prof. Lee know the muddiest points from her on the Minute Papers. She suggests adding Practice Quizzes for every unit and doing the Minute Paper activity at the end of every class session.

Ken

Ken is pleased to learn that Prof. Lee chose to create streaming videos as one of the Content options because he learns better by watching and listening to others explaining new information instead of reading it. He ends up watching the Search Strategies mini-lecture twice just to be sure that he picked up on all the important information it contains. The second time he watches it on YouTube, he changes the playback speed to 1.25× because he finds that Prof. Lee speaks a bit slowly. He has a question about one of the features mentioned in the Academic OneFile video on the morning he is watching and e-mails Prof. Lee about it because he is a bit shy about asking a question in class, in front of his peers. Ken is grateful to get a reply from her in less than an hour that fully addresses his question.

During the Discussion and Review at the beginning of the Search Strategies class session, Ken listens attentively as Prof. Lee answers the students' questions, and he copies down what she says. He does the same during the class discussion of the two review questions. He finds the Comparing Resources and Results activity helpful because his groupmates share some interesting perspectives on the search tools' features that he had not thought of. What Ken likes best about the activity is that Prof. Lee is available to answer questions the moment they arise, and the group has three questions for her during the time they are working.

When it is time for the Minute Paper, he struggles to think of a muddiest point because Prof. Lee addressed his biggest question in her e-mail reply, and she answered the other questions he and his groupmates had during the class session. At the last moment, he thinks of something minor and jots it down, but Prof. Lee does not answer it in her follow-up e-mail. He is not disappointed because she mentioned in class that she would address muddiest points that several students had or that were not clearly stated in the readings or videos. He thinks that his muddiest point was probably outside the scope of what the class needs to learn in the course, so he does not worry about it. Ken completes the Practice Quiz immediately after class and is excited when the quiz tool immediately scores his submission and shows that he answered every question correctly.

The fact that so many students ask questions at the start of the Review and Discussion during the first Critically Evaluating Sources class session is somewhat frustrating to Ken because he thinks that some of the answers to the questions can be found directly in the videos. He is pleased that Prof. Lee decides to turn the questions into a discussion because she modifies each question to get students to think more deeply about the topic. During the Comparing Resources and Results activity, Ken spends most of the time listening to his groupmates debate their evaluations of the sources they are examining. Listening to them makes him think that his evaluations may have only scratched the surface of what the students should be considering as part of the process, and he makes a mental note to be more thorough in the future. When writing the Minute Paper he realizes that he forgot to ask Prof. Lee a question that he had during the group activity and writes that down as his muddiest point, which she addresses in the follow-up e-mail.

Ken finds the discussion at the beginning of the last differentiated class session quite engaging, and he contributes one point to the discussion of the last review question. For Think-Pair-Share, he works with a classmate who sits next to him but whom he has never spoken with before, and they end up in an engrossing discussion about their ideas to address the issue of access to information for members of marginalized groups. They decide to share the other student's idea with the class, and Ken is impressed by the creativity shown in the ideas the other pairs present. When he completes the Practice Quiz the following day, he has one incorrect answer and is glad that an explanation of why another choice is correct is shown right away.

Ken initially plans to write every section of the Research Project. As he is conducting the research by following his planned strategy, he notices that he is jotting down brief notes in separate lines of his notebook and realizes that if he added a few arrows and boxes, it would look like a flowchart. He decides that he might as well submit the Process section as a flowchart since he knows how to use shapes and arrows in Microsoft Word, and the information he would need to fill in the flowchart is already in his notes. He writes the other portions of the final project.

In his feedback on the differentiated units, Ken admits he expected that he would not learn as well without lectures, but he found the mini-lessons to be a better option because he could watch them more than once and pause at any time. He shares that he benefited from the insights of his classmates during the group activities and the discussions. Although he thinks that the work outside of class took a bit more time than if it were readings and homework assignments, he probably learned the material in the differentiated units more quickly and to a deeper level of understanding than the information in the other units. He suggests that all the lectures be replaced by videos in future semesters.

DIFFERENTIATING A ONE-SHOT SESSION

For many academic instruction librarians, a large share of the teaching they do occurs in one-shot sessions where they are invited by subject faculty to present to their students for a single class session or a portion of one. With such limited time, it may seem difficult to differentiate a one-shot. However, adopting a flipped classroom structure for a one-shot can make differentiated instruction feasible and help students maximize what they learn.

These five steps should be followed when planning differentiated instruction for a one-shot session:

1. Determine learning outcomes.
2. Plan how to differentiate Content. Create new Content learning objects, if needed.
3. Plan how to differentiate Process. Create new Process learning objects, if needed.
4. Decide whether to include a formative assessment Product. Create new Product learning objects, if needed.
5. Create a lesson plan.

1. Determine Learning Outcomes

Because a one-shot spans only a limited time, identifying the learning outcomes you expect students will be able to reasonably achieve during that time can help focus your planning so that the Content and Process learning objects are narrowly tailored to the outcomes. Work with the course instructor to identify the learning needs that should be addressed by the one-shot. Will the students be working on a particular assignment that involves research? What does the course instructor believe you should cover during the one-shot? What research tools or resources are most important for the students to become familiar with?

As always, the learning outcomes should be specific and measurable or observable. They will help you in deciding what to include in the differentiated Content and in planning active learning Process exercises for use during the class session. Even though you will not be grading the students using a summative assessment, you can still use a formative assessment to evaluate students' mastery of the learning outcomes as part of your differentiated one-shot, as discussed in the fourth step.

2. Plan How to Differentiate Content

Academic instruction librarians teaching one-shots often use an in-class lecture or mini-lecture as the method of delivering the new Content to students. Although this direct instruction can be an effective way to get students engaged with the material, it consumes valuable minutes from the limited time you may have with them. Eliminating direct instruction by employing a flipped classroom approach to the one-shot can free up face-to-face time for active learning Process exercises where students can work toward making sense of the material by putting what you are teaching them into practice.

You can identify existing Content that presents the material associated with the learning outcomes or create new Content and ask the course instructor to assign that Content to students to complete before the day of the one-shot. You can find or create a variety of differentiated Content so that students have a choice of how they will engage with the material in advance of the one-shot. If learning how to use particular electronic resources or print resources is among the learning goals, consider including vendor-created streaming video tutorials or create tutorials so that you will not need to demonstrate how to use these resources in class.

Because you will not be administering a preassessment to the students and are not familiar with their learning styles, you should try to include options that are appealing to several of the learning styles described in Figure 4.1 (page 47). Two or three well chosen Content techniques, from among those described in Chapter Four, should be sufficient to accommodate the learning preferences of many different types of learners. Make sure that all of the information in the Content you provide is directly tied to one of the learning outcomes. Anything that is not should be cut.

3. Plan How to Differentiate Process

Now that the students will presumably be engaging with the Content in advance of the one-shot, you can plan to dedicate the time you have with the class to Process activities, in keeping with the flipped classroom model. Your selection of Process active learning exercises, such as those described in Chapter Five, is limited only by the mastery goals established in the learning outcomes and the amount of time you have with the students. You should identify Process techniques that will help students efficiently build the knowledge and skills you are teaching them. If a suitable Process technique can be done with students working in small groups or individually, offer both options so that students can choose which best suits their learning preferences.

If you would like to talk about the material presented in the Content for a few minutes before beginning an active learning exercise, you can open the class session with the Review and Discussion activity described in Chapter Five. Be mindful to stick to the parameters of the technique in order to avoid presenting a mini-lesson that repeats what was in the Content. For examples of how to use this activity, read about Prof. Lee's implementation of it in the "Review and Discussion" and "The Differentiated Units" sections earlier in this chapter.

If appropriate, you can turn an exercise into a game by rewarding the student or group who completes the activity first with a small prize, such as candy or a promotional item from a vendor that was given to the library for free. Promotional items given in limited quantities, usually of a higher cost than a pen or notepad, make good prizes. Making an exercise into a game where there is a clear winner or winning group appeals to competitive learners.

4. Decide Whether to Include a Formative Assessment Product

It is reasonable to think that, because you will be working with a class for only a limited amount of time and you will not be grading the students, there is no need to include an assessment Product for your one-shot. Nonetheless, including a formative assessment can help the students gauge how well they understood the material that was taught in the Content and that was put into practice in the Process activities. A formative assessment can also assist you with determining the effectiveness of the one-shot and identifying ways to improve the lesson if you happen to teach it again in future semesters.

A Practice Quiz delivered through your institution's learning management system or one of the online quiz tools recommended in Chapter Six can be completed by students after the one-shot and be set up to provide immediate feedback upon submission. Not only will the students get a sense for how successfully they mastered what was taught, but you will have access to the full set of responses to review. When analyzing the results, you may find that many students incorrectly answered the same question or questions, indicating that you may need to dedicate more time to clarifying the related material in the future. If time permits, you can also use a student response system, such as clickers or an online tool, to do a quick practice quiz at the end of the one-shot class session.

Reserving a few minutes at the end of the one-shot for students to complete a Minute Paper exercise is a quick way to reveal whether any aspects of the one-shot Content or Process need improvement. If many students write down the same muddiest point, you may need to revisit how that point is addressed in the Content and applied in the Process activities. Be sure to follow up with the class by e-mailing them to clarify the most commonly repeated muddiest points because this feedback will improve their understanding of what you intended them to learn.

You may want to ask the students to e-mail you a 3× Summarization after the one-shot to get a fuller picture of what they learned during the lesson than what you might get from a Practice Quiz or Minute Paper. You can either describe the formative assessment at the end of the one-shot or e-mail the students an explanation, making it easy for them to reply with their summarizations. Keep in mind that providing students feedback is a necessary part of the formative assessment process, and you will need to give the students individual feedback if you follow this approach.

5. Create a Lesson Plan

Preparing a lesson plan is critical for a one-shot session because your time with students is limited, and you do not have the option of completing the lesson at the beginning of the next class session, as you do if you are teaching an information literacy course. It is best to include as many pertinent details as you can in a lesson plan so that, during the session, you can quickly reference all the information in one place. In addition to a schedule for the face-to-face time with the class that identifies the Process active learning exercises, your lesson plan should contain information about the course and any assignments related to the one-shot, the learning outcomes, a listing of the Content choices, and any materials you may need to bring, and, if applicable, it should identify any postclass formative assessment that you plan to use.

Figure 7.4 is a sample lesson plan for a one-shot in an introductory writing course. For this one-shot, the course instructor has asked the instructional librarian to provide an overview of the research process to her class one week before the students need to submit their proposed topic for a seven-page research paper. She expects students to find and cite five scholarly articles for their papers, so they need to be able to distinguish scholarly sources from popular sources.

Because of the limited time, the librarian decides that it is best to focus on searching in the library's catalog and aggregated search platform. After determining the learning outcomes stated in the lesson plan, he decides that, instead of a lecture on the search process, he should ask the instructor to assign students to either read a guide that the team of instructional librarians wrote on the fundamentals of researching or watch a video on the library's Web site that explains the same material, offering two differentiated Content choices. He also asks the instructor to assign two additional videos on using the library catalog and its aggregated search platform. The instructor gives students the assignment, and the librarian e-mails the class several days ahead of time to explain the one-shot and the purpose of the assignment.

During the one-shot, the librarian plans to spend the first 20 minutes doing a Review and Discussion with the class and prepares seven review questions for the class to discuss after students have an opportunity to ask questions about the material in the Content. He will then give a seven- to ten-minute lecture on the differences between scholarly and popular sources, using a Google Slides presentation with mostly images and minimal text

---

One-Shot Lesson Plan

Course title (Instructor): English Composition I (Garber)

Lesson title: Research Fundamentals

Related assignment: 7-page research paper on a topic of the student's choosing, citing five scholarly articles

Learning outcomes: Students should be able to…
- explain the basic research process.
- explain how to identify scholarly sources.
- conduct searches in the library catalog and aggregated search platform.

Content: Choice of: 1) research process readings, or 2) research process video lesson; Required: videos on using library catalog and aggregated search

Materials needed: Activity worksheets; Loaner laptop; Pens

Schedule (75 minutes)

Time	Activity (type)
0-20	Review & Discussion of the Basic Research Process (Process)
20-40	Lecture & Discussion: Scholarly v. Popular Sources (Content/Process)
40-60	Identifying Scholarly Sources (Small-group Process)
60-70	Individual Research (Process)
70-75	Minute Paper (Product – formative assessment)

Figure 7.4 One-Shot Lesson Plan

to accommodate visual learners. The discussion portion will be a whole-group activity where screenshots of full-text scholarly and popular articles found using the library's aggregated search platform will be displayed, and the class will work together to determine what type of source it is. The class will then break into groups of three or four and spend 20 minutes searching for articles on a topic assigned by the librarian and deciding whether they are scholarly or popular. Students will then spend 10 minutes working alone on searching for scholarly articles for a paper topic they are considering before completing a Minute Paper during the last few minutes of the session. The librarian chooses this mix of whole-group discussions, small-group work, and individual work to accommodate the learning preferences of read-write, aural, collaborative, dependent, and independent students at different times during the one-shot.

CONCLUSION

Given the popularity of differentiated instruction in primary and secondary education, you are likely already teaching students who have experienced its benefits earlier in their education. As the composition of student populations in higher education grows more diverse, you will continue to encounter greater variety in students' backgrounds, cultural norms, and cultural expectations that influence their learning styles and interactions with instructors and peers. Throughout this book, you have learned how the adoption of differentiated instruction enables you to accommodate the learning needs of students with different backgrounds, readiness levels, interests, and learning styles. By identifying clear learning outcomes and offering students choices for the learning objects they use to engage with new material, make sense of what they are learning, test their own understanding, and eventually show their mastery of the material, you can maximize each student's opportunity to succeed in your courses or get the most out of the one-shot sessions you teach. Incorporating critical information literacy concepts into your instruction can further help students become active agents in their learning by questioning the power structures present in the production and dissemination of information.

Adopting differentiated instruction, like any change in your teaching, will take some time to adjust to, but the benefits to your students' learning will make the endeavor worthwhile. By putting into practice the guidance presented in Chapters Three through Seven and making use of the recommended resources for differentiating Content, Process, and Product, you can more easily transform your information literacy courses and one-shots to better accommodate the learning needs of all your students. As you embark on your first experience with differentiated instruction, be sure to keep track of what worked well and what needs to be changed—and return to this book regularly to refresh yourself on the tips and guidance offered for each phase of differentiation. Good luck!

References

American Library Association. (1989). *Presidential Committee on Information Literacy. Final report.* Retrieved from http://www.ala.org/acrl /publications/whitepapers/presidential

Association of College and Research Libraries. (2015). *Framework for information literacy for higher education.* Chicago: Association of College and Research Libraries.

Association of College and Research Libraries. (2000). *Information literacy competency standards for higher education.* Chicago: Association of College and Research Libraries.

Auyeung, P., & Sands, J. (1996). A cross-cultural study of the learning style of accounting students. *Accounting and Finance, 36*(2), 261–274. doi:10.1111/j.1467-629X.1996.tb00310.x

Aydin, B., & Demirer, V. (2016). Flipping the drawbacks of flipped classroom: Effective tools and recommendations. *Journal of Educational and Instructional Studies in the World, 6*(1), 33–40. doi:10.1186 /s41239-016-0032-z

Bergmann, J., & Sams, A. (2012). *Flip your classroom: Reach every student in every class every day.* Eugene, OR: International Society for Technology in Education.

Brookhart, S. M. (2013). *How to create and use rubrics for formative assessment and grading.* Alexandria, VA: Association for Supervision and Curriculum Development.

Butler, M., & Van Lowe, K. (2010). Using differentiated instruction in teacher education. *International Journal for Mathematics Teaching and Learning*. Retrieved from http://www.cimt.org.uk/journal/butler.pdf

Chamberlin, M., & Powers, R. (2010). The promise of differentiated instruction for enhancing the mathematical understandings of college students. *Teaching Mathematics and Its Applications*, *29*(3), 113–139. doi:10.1093/teamat/hrq006

Coffield, F., Moseley, D., Hall, E., & Ecclestone, K. (2004). *Learning styles and pedagogy in post-16 learning: A systematic and critical review*. London: Learning and Skills Research Centre.

Cope, J. (2010). Information literacy and social power. In Accardi, M. T., Drabinski, E., & Kumbier, A. (Eds.), *Critical library instruction: Theories and methods* (pp. 13–27). Duluth, MN: Library Juice Press.

Doherty, J. J. (2007). No shhing: Giving voice to the silenced: An essay in support of critical information literacy. *Library Philosophy and Practice*, Paper 133, 1–8. Retrieved from http://digitalcommons.unl.edu/libphilprac/133

Doherty, J. J., & Ketchner, K. (2005). Empowering the intentional learner: A critical theory for information literacy instruction. *Library Philosophy and Practice*, *8*(1), 1–10.

Dosch, M., & Zidon, M. (2014). "The course fit us": Differentiated instruction in the college classroom. *International Journal of Teaching and Learning in Higher Education*, *26*(3), 343–357.

Dunaway, M. (2011). Web 2.0 and critical information literacy. *Public Services Quarterly*, *7*(3–4), 149–157. doi:10.1080/15228959.2011.622628

Elmborg, J. (2006). Critical information literacy: Implications for instructional practice. *The Journal of Academic Librarianship*, *32*(2), 192–199. doi:10.1016/j.acalib.2005.12.004

Elmborg, J. (2012). Critical information literacy: Definitions and challenges. In Wetzel, C., & Bruch, C. (Eds.), *Transforming Information literacy programs: Intersecting frontiers of self, library culture, and campus community* (pp. 75–95). Chicago: Association of College and Research Libraries.

Foasberg, N. M. (2015). From standards to frameworks for IL: How the ACRL Framework addresses critiques of the Standards. *portal: Libraries and the Academy, 15*(4), 699–717.

Grasha, A. F. (1990). Using traditional versus naturalistic approaches to assessing learning styles in college teaching. *Journal of Excellence in College Teaching, 1*(1), 23–38.

Guild, P. (1994). The culture/learning style connection. *Educational Leadership, 51*(8), 16–21.

Hall, R. (2010). Public praxis: A vision for critical information literacy in public libraries. *Public Library Quarterly, 29*(2), 162–175. doi:10.1080/01616841003776383

Hamdan, N., McKnight, P., McKnight, K., & Arfstrom, K. (2013). *A review of flipped learning.* Retrieved from https://flippedlearning.org/wp-content/uploads/2016/07/LitReview_FlippedLearning.pdf

House, R. J., Hanges, P. J., Javidan, M., Dorfman, P. W., & Gupta, V. (2004). *Culture, leadership, and organizations: The GLOBE study of 62 societies.* Thousand Oaks, CA: Sage.

Jacobson, M.H.S. (2001). A primer on learning styles: Reaching every student. *Seattle University Law Review, 25*(1), 139–178.

James, W. B., & Gardner, D. L. (1995). Learning styles: Implications for distance learning. *New Directions for Adult and Continuing Education, 67*, 19–32. doi:10.1002/ace.36719956705

Kapitzke, C. (2001). Information literacy: The changing library. *Journal of Adolescent & Adult Literacy, 44*(5), 450.

Kolb, A. Y., & Kolb, D. A. (2005). Learning styles and learning spaces: Enhancing experiential learning in higher education. *Academy of*

Management Learning & Education, *4*(2), 193–212. doi:10.5465/amle.2005.17268566

Lage, M. J., Platt, G. J., & Treglia, M. (2000). Inverting the classroom: A gateway to creating an inclusive learning environment. *The Journal of Economic Education*, *31*(1), 30–43. doi:10.1080/00220480009596759

Livingston, D. (2006). Differentiated instruction and assessment in the college classroom. *Reaching through Teaching: A Journal of the Practice, Philosophy and Scholarship of College Teaching*, *16*(2), 17–31.

Luke, A., & Kapitzke, C. (1999). Literacies and libraries: Archives and cybraries. *Pedagogy, Culture & Society*, *7*(3), 467–491. doi:10.1080/14681369900200066

Marshall, R. K. (2006). An instrument to measure information competency. *Journal of Literacy and Technology*, *6*(1), 1–27.

McSpadden, K. (2015, May 14). You now have a shorter attention span than a goldfish. *Time*. Retrieved from http://time.com/3858309/attention-spans-goldfish/

Packard, J. (2011). The impact of racial diversity in the classroom: Activating the sociological imagination. *Teaching Sociology*, *41*(2), 144–58. doi:10.1177/0092055X12451716

Papadopoulos, C., & Roman, A. S. (2010). Implementing an inverted classroom model in engineering statics: Initial results. In *Proceedings, American Society for Engineering Education Annual Conference & Exhibition* (pp. 15.679.1–15.679.27). Washington, DC: American Society for Engineering Education.

Rinne, N. A. (2017). The new Framework: A truth-less construction just waiting to be scrapped? *Reference Services Review*, *45*(1), 54–66. doi:10.1108/RSR-06-2016-0039

Santangelo, T., & Tomlinson, C. A. (2009). The application of differentiated instruction in postsecondary environments: Benefits, challenges, and future directions. *International Journal of Teaching and Learning in Higher Education, 20*(3), 307–323.

Santangelo, T., & Tomlinson, C. A. (2012). Teacher educators' perceptions and use of differentiated instruction practices: An exploratory investigation. *Action in Teacher Education, 34*(4), 309–327. doi:10.1080/01626620.2012.717032

Seale, M. (2010). Information literacy standards and the politics of knowledge production: Using user-generated content to incorporate critical pedagogy. In Accardi, M. T., Drabinski, E., & Kumbier, A. (Eds.), *Critical library instruction: Theories and methods* (pp. 221–235). Duluth, MN: Library Juice Press.

Smith, L. (2013). Towards a model of critical information literacy instruction for the development of political agency. *Journal of Information Literacy, 7*(2), 15–32. doi:10.11645/7.2.1809

Swanson, T. A. (2004). A radical step: Implementing a critical information literacy model. *portal: Libraries and the Academy, 4*(2), 259–273. doi:10.1353/pla.2004.0038

Swanson, T. A. (2005). Applying a critical pedagogical perspective to information literacy standards. *Community & Junior College Libraries, 12*(4), 65–77. doi:10.1300/J107v12n04_08

Tempelaar, D. T., Rienties, B., Giesbers, B., & van der Loeff, S. S. (2013). Cultural differences in learning dispositions. In Van den Bossche, P., Gijselaers, W. H., & Milter, R. G. (Eds.), *Facilitating learning in the 21st century: Leading through technology, diversity and authenticity* (pp. 3–30). Dordrecht, The Netherlands: Springer.

Tewell, E. (2015). A decade of critical information literacy: A review of the literature. *Communications in Information Literacy, 9*(1), 24–43.

Wynd, W. R., & Bozman, C. S. (1996). Student learning style: A segmentation strategy for higher education. *Journal of Education for Business, 71*(4), 232–235. doi:10.1080/08832323.1996.10116790

Yamazaki, Y., & Kayes, D. C. (2007). Expatriate learning: Exploring how Japanese managers adapt in the United States. *International Journal of Human Resource Management, 18*(8), 1373–1395. doi:10.1080/09585190701502521

Zapalska, A., & Dabb, H. (2002). Learning styles. *Journal of Teaching in International Business, 13*(3–4), 77–97. doi:10.1300/J066v13n03_06

Zappe, S., Leicht, R., Messner, J., Litzinger, T., & Lee, H. W. (2009). "Flipping" the classroom to explore active learning in a large undergraduate course. In *Proceedings, American Society for Engineering Education Annual Conference & Exhibition* (pp 14.1385.1–14.1385.21). Washington, DC: American Society for Engineering Education.

Index

Note: Page numbers followed by *t* indicate tables and *f* indicate figures.

About the Author

Alex Berrio Matamoros is Manager of Knowledge Management at Debevoise & Plimpton LLP, an international law firm. During his time as associate law library professor and emerging technologies librarian at the City University of New York (CUNY) School of Law, he was a recipient of the 2016 CUNY Excellence in Technology Award and the 75th Anniversary Distinguished Leadership Award of the Law Library Association of Greater New York. In recognition of his service to the field of law librarianship, Berrio Matamoros is profiled in *Celebrating Diversity: A Legacy of Minority Leadership in the American Association of Law Libraries*, second edition.